Language Arts

Activity Book

Book Staff and Contributors

Beth Zemble *Director, Alternative Learning Strategies; Director, English Language Arts*
Marianne Murphy *Content Specialist*
Anna Day *Senior Instructional Designer*
Cheryl Howard, Jenn Marrewa, Frances Suazo *Instructional Designers*
Mary Beck Desmond *Senior Text Editor*
Ron Stanley, Jill Tunick *Text Editors*
Suzanne Montazer *Creative Director, Print and ePublishing*
Jayoung Cho *Senior Print Visual Designer*
Chris Byrne, Raymond MacDonald *Print Visual Designers*
Stephanie Williams *Cover Designer*
Amy Eward *Senior Manager, Writers*
Susan Raley *Senior Manager, Editors*
Seth Herz *Director, Program Management Grades K–8*

Maria Szalay *Senior Vice President, Product Development*
John Holdren *Senior Vice President, Content and Curriculum*
David Pelizzari *Vice President, Content and Curriculum*
Kim Barcas *Vice President, Creative*
Laura Seuschek *Vice President, Instructional Design and Evaluation & Research*
Aaron Hall *Vice President, Program Management*

Lisa Dimaio Iekel *Production Manager*
John Agnone *Director of Publications*

Credits

All illustrations © K12 unless otherwise noted
Ladybug. © Eyewire/Getty Images

About K12 Inc.

K12 Inc., a technology-based education company, is the nation's leading provider of proprietary curriculum and online education programs to students in grades K–12. K12 provides its curriculum and academic services to online schools, traditional classrooms, blended school programs, and directly to families. K12 Inc. also operates the K12 International Academy, an accredited, diploma-granting online private school serving students worldwide. K12's mission is to provide any child the curriculum and tools to maximize success in life, regardless of geographic, financial, or demographic circumstances. K12 Inc. is accredited by CITA. More information can be found at www.K12.com.

978-1-60153-166-7
Printed by RR Donnelley & Sons, Willard, Ohio, USA, April 2013, Lot 042013

Contents

Literature & Comprehension

Furry Friends

Flying Friends

Poetry

Classics for All Ages

A Weed is a Flower

Winds and Wings

Writing Skills

Complete Sentences

Write Sentences

Kinds of Sentences

Write Friendly Letters

Singular and Plural Nouns

ents!

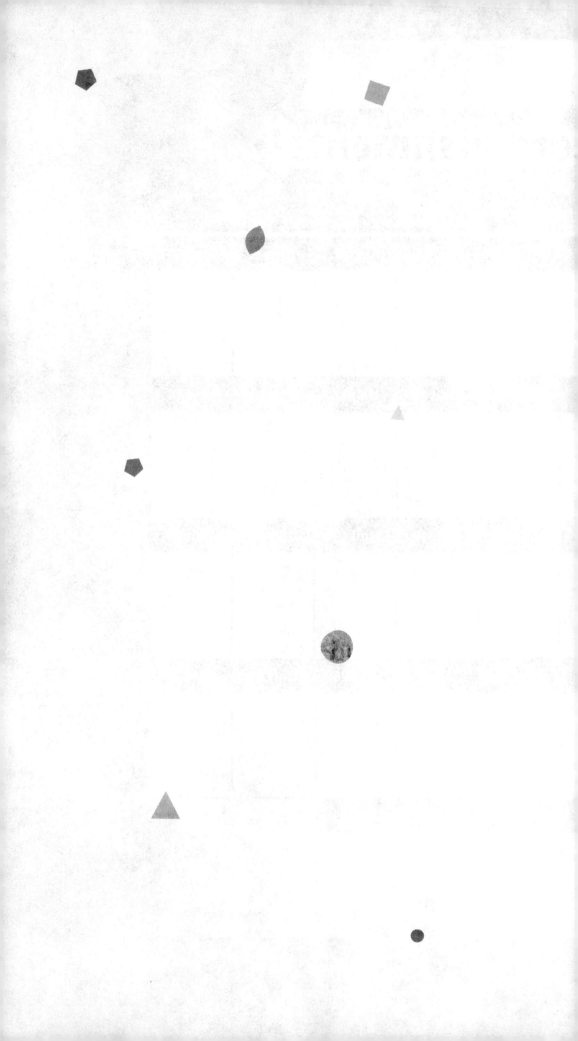

Name

My Accomplishments!

SPELLING

Unit 1	Unit 2	Unit 3	Unit 4	Unit 5	Unit 6	Unit 7	Unit 8

Unit 9	Unit 10	Unit 11	Unit 12	Unit 13	Unit 14	Unit 15	Unit 16

Unit 17	Unit 18	Unit 19	Unit 20	Unit 21	Unit 22	Unit 23	Unit 24

Unit 25	Unit 26	Unit 27	Unit 28	Unit 29	Unit 30	Unit 31	Unit 32

Unit 33	Unit 34	Unit 35	Unit 36

Language Arts Orange

Name ....

My Accomplishments!

WRITING SKILLS

Unit 1	Unit 2	Unit 3	Unit 4	Unit 5	Unit 6	Unit 7	Unit 8

Unit 9	Unit 10	Unit 11	Unit 12	Unit 13	Unit 14	Unit 15	Unit 16

Unit 17	Unit 18	Unit 19	Unit 20	Unit 21	Unit 22	Unit 23	Unit 24

Unit 25	Unit 26	Unit 27	Unit 28	Unit 29	Unit 30	Unit 31	Unit 32

Unit 33	Unit 34	Unit 35	Unit 36

Language Arts Orange

Name

My Accomplishments!

Unit 1	Unit 2	Unit 3	Unit 4	Unit 5	Unit 6	Unit 7	Unit 8

Unit 9	Unit 10	Unit 11	Unit 12	Unit 13	Unit 14	Unit 15	Unit 16

Unit 17	Unit 18	Unit 19	Unit 20	Unit 21	Unit 22	Unit 23	Unit 24

Unit 25	Unit 26	Unit 27	Unit 28	Unit 29	Unit 30	Unit 31	Unit 32

Unit 33	Unit 34	Unit 35	Unit 36

Language Arts Orange

Literature & Comprehension

Paste the story boxes in the correct order.

Beginning

Middle

End

Introduce "The Hound and the Hare"
Beginning, Middle, and End

Write what happens in the story first, next, and finally.

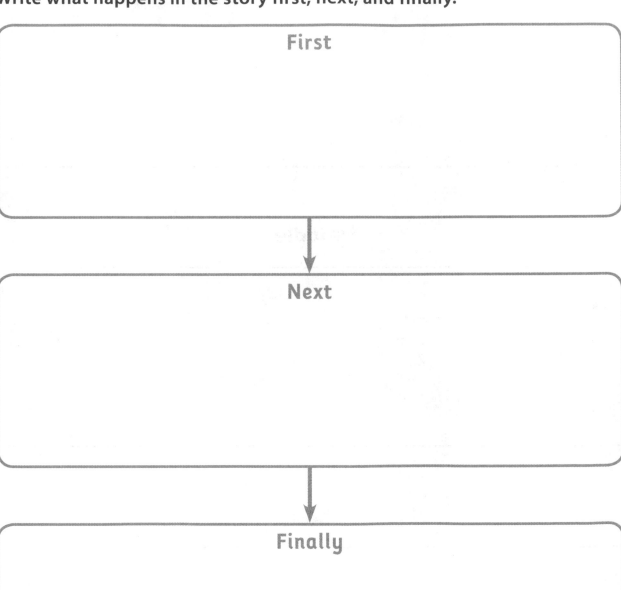

First

Next

Finally

Review "The Hound and the Hare"
Write a New Ending

Write a new ending to the story. What does the Hound say to the Hare in your ending?

_____

_____

_____

_____

_____

_____

_____

_____

LITERATURE & COMPREHENSION

Introduce "The Life of a Butterfly"
Main Idea and Supporting Details

Complete each sentence. Use facts from the nonfiction article.

LITERATURE & COMPREHENSION

> **Main Idea**
> Newly hatched caterpillars

Supporting Detail
Caterpillars eat

Supporting Detail
A monarch caterpillar can grow to be

Supporting Detail
A caterpillar molts

Review "The Life of a Butterfly"
Main Idea and Supporting Details

Complete each sentence. Use facts from the nonfiction article.

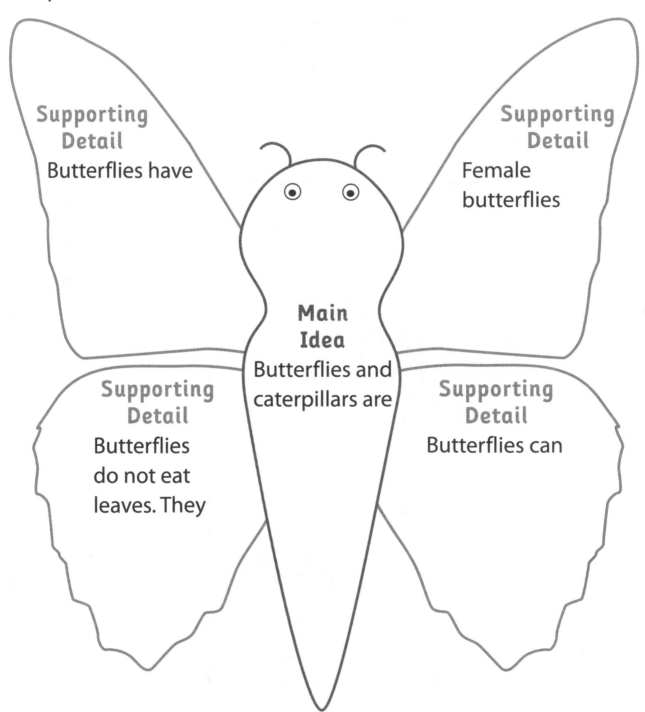

Supporting Detail
Butterflies have

Supporting Detail
Female butterflies

Main Idea
Butterflies and caterpillars are

Supporting Detail
Butterflies do not eat leaves. They

Supporting Detail
Butterflies can

Introduce "I See a Honeybee"
Main Idea and Supporting Details

Complete each sentence. Use facts from the nonfiction article.

Supporting Detail

Worker bees store

Supporting Detail

Worker bees build

Main Idea

Worker bees do

Supporting Detail

Worker bees take care of

Supporting Detail

When the queen bee dies, worker bees put

Review "I See a Honeybee"
Main Idea and Supporting Details

Complete each sentence. Use facts from the nonfiction article.

Supporting Detail

A dance in a circle means

Supporting Detail

The scout faces in the direction

Main Idea

The scout tells the other honeybees where to find nectar by

Supporting Detail

The other bees in the hive feel the scout's movements and know

Supporting Detail

A dance in the shape of an eight means

Introduce Creepy-Crawly Poems
Find the Rhymes

Write two pairs of words that rhyme in the poem "Caterpillars."

1.

2.

Write your own word that rhymes with each word.

3. chew _____

4. grow _____

5. by _____

6. do _____

Introduce Poems About Feelings
How Does the Speaker Feel?

Complete the chart to show how the speaker in "Last Laugh" feels.

What the Speaker Says

↓

What the Speaker Feels

↓

Why I Think This

Introduce More Poems About Feelings
Understand Feelings in Poetry

Complete the chart to show how the speaker in "Hope" feels.

What the Speaker Says		What I Know		How the Speaker Feels
	+		=	

LANGUAGE ARTS ORANGE

Introduce "The Fox and the Grapes"
Character

Answer the questions about "The Fox and the Grapes."

1. What does the fox **say** at the beginning of the story?

   _____

2. What does the fox **do** in the middle of the story?

   _____

3. What does the fox **say** at the end of the story?

   _____

4. What does the fox **do** at the end of the story?

   _____

5. Why does the fox say the grapes are sour?

   _____

6. How would you describe the fox?

   _____

LITERATURE & COMPREHENSION

Review "The Fox and the Grapes"
This Happened to Me

Read the moral, and then answer the questions.

> The moral of the story is
> "It's easy to dislike what you cannot have."

1. Tell this moral in your own words.

   _____

   _____

   _____

   _____

   _____

2. Write about a time when you wanted something that you could not have. Tell how you felt and what you did.

   _____

   _____

   _____

Introduce "The Goose and the Golden Eggs"
Cause and Effect

Complete the chart. Write the causes and effects in "The Goose and the Golden Eggs." The first one has been done for you.

> A **cause** is why something happens.
> An **effect** is what happens as a result of a cause.

Cause	Effect
The man sells the golden eggs at the market.	→ **The man makes money.**
The man saves his money.	→
	→ The man wants to kill the goose.
The man kills the goose.	→

Review "The Goose and the Golden Eggs"

Character Traits

Write a character trait for each example of what the man in the story says or does.

What the Man Says or Does	Character Trait
The man saves his money and slowly becomes rich.	
The man says to himself, "I wish that I were rich now."	
The man kills the goose.	

Introduce "The Pied Piper of Hamelin" (B)
Main Character Web

Write clues about the Pied Piper's character from both parts of the story. Then, think about the clues and write a trait for the Pied Piper in the center.

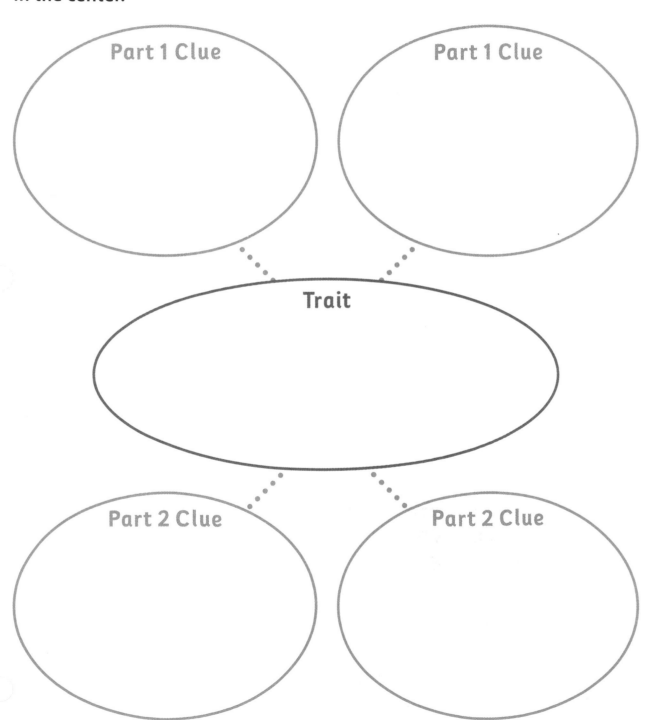

Part 1 Clue

Part 1 Clue

Trait

Part 2 Clue

Part 2 Clue

Review "The Pied Piper of Hamelin"
Cause and Effect

Complete the chart to show the causes and effects in the story. Fill in the boxes in the order shown by the arrows. The first one has been done for you.

The Pied Piper says **he can drive the rats out of Hamelin.**

→

The Mayor agrees to pay the Pied Piper

↓

The Pied Piper plays his pipe and

←

The Pied Piper says he wants his money. But, the Mayor says

↓

The Pied Piper plays his pipe. The children of Hamelin

→

No one in Hamelin is allowed to

Review "The Bremen Town Musicians"

Cause and Effect

Match each cause with its effect.

Cause	Effect
The owners of the animals want to kill them.	The animals go off to Bremen together.
The Donkey invites the animals he meets to join his band.	The animals run away.
The animals want to eat the supper of the robbers.	The Cat scratches him, the Dog bites him, the Donkey kicks him, and the Cock crows.
A robber creeps back into the house.	The animals make their loudest music and scare off the robbers.
The robber thinks a witch, a man with a knife, and a giant are in the house.	The robbers run away, and the animals stay in the house.

Introduce "The Bremen Town Musicians" (B)

Describe Characters

Write clues from the story about the donkey.

Part 1	Part 2
What the Donkey says:	What the Donkey says:
What the Donkey does:	What the Donkey does:
What other characters say about the Donkey:	What other characters say about the Donkey:

Introduce *A Weed is a Flower*

Main Idea and Supporting Details

Use information from the first part of *A Weed is a Flower* to complete the sentence in each box.

> **Main idea**
> George Washington Carver liked to

Supporting Detail
George asked

Supporting Detail
If his plants weren't growing well, George

Supporting Detail
George left the Carvers' farm because he wanted

Explore *A Weed is a Flower*
Main Idea and Supporting Details

Use information from the second part of *A Weed is a Flower* to complete the sentence in each oval.

Supporting Detail
Dr. Carver showed people that these crops could be used to

Main idea
George asked people to

Supporting Detail
Dr. Carver said these crops were better for

Supporting Detail
These crops became

Review *A Weed is a Flower*
Main Idea and Supporting Details

Complete the sentence in each box.

Main Idea
Even at the end of his life, George Washington Carver still

Supporting Detail
Dr. Carver took care of himself by

Supporting Detail
Dr. Carver worked every day in

Supporting Detail
Dr. Carver continued to help people by

Review *A Weed is a Flower*
Summarize

Write a summary of *A Weed is a Flower*.

_____

_____

_____

_____

_____

_____

_____

_____

_____

Introduce "Something Told the Wild Geese"

Sensory Language

Write words from the poem that describe things you can see, hear, taste, smell, or feel. Write words for late summer in the first column. Write words for winter in the second column.

Late Summer	Winter

LITERATURE & COMPREHENSION

Introduce "Who Has Seen the Wind?"
Images of the Wind

The poet uses imagery to describe the wind. Write your own images of the wind in the web.

LITERATURE & COMPREHENSION

leaves hang trembling

leaves bow down their heads

The wind

Introduce "Windy Nights"

Compare Two Poems

Choose two poems from the book to compare. Write their titles on the lines. Complete the Venn diagram.

Title _____   Title _____

_____   _____

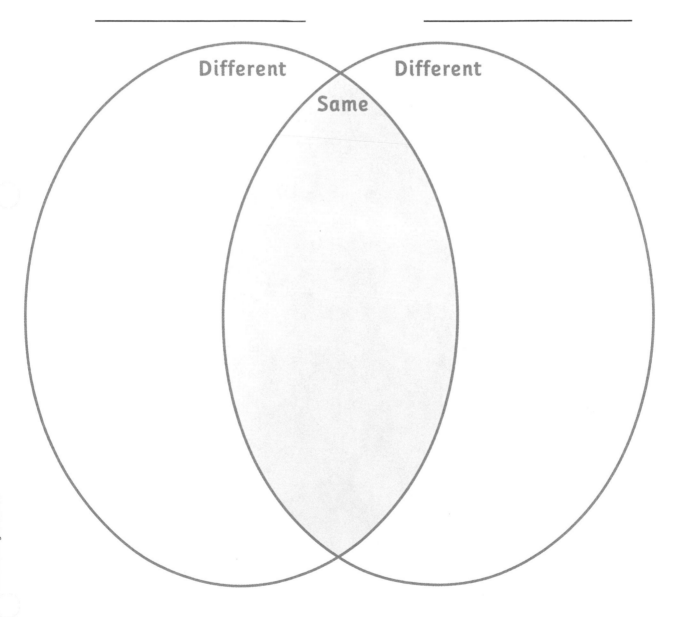

Different   Different

Same

LITERATURE & COMPREHENSION

Introduce "Living with Latin"

Use Evidence to Answer Questions

Write the answer to the question. Then, write the sentence from the text that supports your answer.

1. How is Latin part of English today?

    My answer: _____

    _____

    Sentence from the text that supports my answer: _____

    _____

    _____

2. What Latin words does the word *vacation* come from?

    My answer: _____

    _____

    Sentence from the text that supports my answer: _____

    _____

    _____

LITERATURE & COMPREHENSION

Review "Living with Latin"
Main Idea and Supporting Details

Complete the chart. Write the main idea in the top box. Use facts from the article to fill in the supporting details.

Main Idea

Supporting Detail

Supporting Detail

Supporting Detail

Introduce "Gods and Spirits of Ancient Rome"
Make Inferences

Fill in each box to make an inference about Minerva.

What I Read	What I Think	My Inference
The Romans wanted Minerva's help with	I think that	The Romans believed that these things

\+ =

LITERATURE & COMPREHENSION

Review "Gods and Spirits of Ancient Rome"
Make Inferences

Complete the chart. To fill in the boxes, use page 17 from the article.

What the Text Says		What I Know		My Inference
The Romans honored their spirits by giving them	+	I think these things are	=	I think the Romans gave spirits these gifts because

Introduce "Clytie"

Why "Clytie" Is a Myth

Fill in the parts of the sunflower.

"Clytie" is a
myth because
it explains how

Magical
Character

Magical
Character

Magical
Character

Review "Clytie"

Make Inferences

Use the story and your own ideas to answer the questions.

1. How do the gods feel about Clytie?

   _____

2. What do the gods do for Clytie?

   _____

   _____

3. What do you do when you feel sorry for someone?

   _____

   _____

4. Why do you think the gods change Clytie?

   _____

   _____

   _____

LITERATURE & COMPREHENSION

Introduce "Pandora's Box"

Why "Pandora's Box" Is a Myth

Draw a circle around the parts of "Pandora's Box" that make the story a myth.

LITERATURE & COMPREHENSION

the gods

a mysterious box with a cord around it

Pandora's good health

ugly pain and sorrow creatures

explains how hope came into the world

Pandora's beauty

explains how sorrow and pain came into the world

Pandora's wit

beautiful Hope creature

Explore "Pandora's Box"
Make Inferences

Choose the answer.

1. How does Hope make Pandora feel?

    A. frightened   **C.** better

    B. sad   **D.** angry

2. Where does Hope go?

    A. back inside the box

    B. to the king of the gods

    C. to Pandora's mother

    D. wherever pain and sorrow go

3. What does Hope bring to people who are sick and sad?

    A. comfort   **C.** sorrow

    B. pain   **D.** fear

4. Why is Hope inside the box with pain and sorrow?

    A. Pandora puts her there so she can always have Hope.

    B. Hope helps people feel better when they are hurting and sad.

    C. Hope wants to live with Pandora forever.

    D. Pandora is angry with Hope, so she locks Hope in.

Review "Pandora's Box"

Theme in "Pandora's Box"

Explore the theme of "Pandora's Box."

1. In your own words, write the theme from the story in the box.

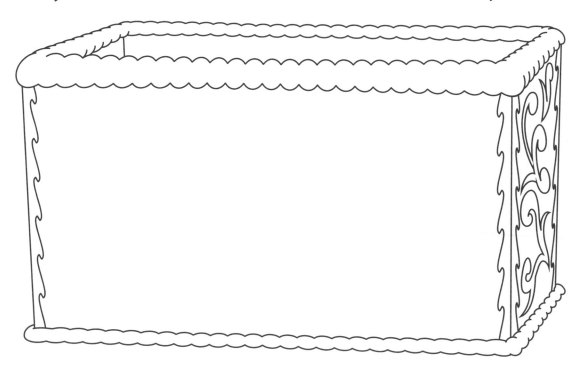

2. Draw a picture of something that happened in your life that shows this theme.

LITERATURE & COMPREHENSION

Introduce "Echo"

Why "Echo" Is a Myth

Answer the questions.

1. Who is the magical character in "Echo"?

   _____

   _____

2. How do you know this character is magical?

   _____

   _____

3. What does the myth explain?

   _____

   _____

4. Why do you think the ancient Romans made a myth to explain echoes?

   _____

   _____

Review "Echo"

Compare Roman Myths

Choose two of the myths "Clytie," "Pandora's Box," or "Echo." Fill in the graphic organizer to show how the myths are the same and how they are different.

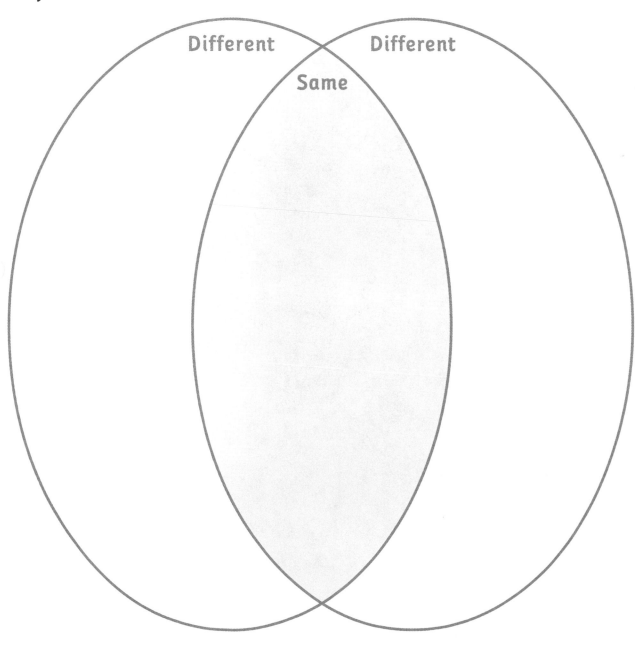

Different   Different

Same

Myth: _____   Myth: _____

Introduce "A Day in Ancient Rome" (B)
Know, Wonder, Learn

Complete the chart with what you know, wonder about, and learn from your reading.

Know	Wonder	Learn

LITERATURE & COMPREHENSION

Introduce "Androcles and the Lion"
Character Traits

Write a character trait for Androcles next to his picture. Write support from the story in the circles.

Support from Story

Support from Story

Trait of Androcles

Support from Story

Explore "Androcles and the Lion"
Choices and Consequences

Complete the chart.

Androcles's Choice	What Androcles Chooses	Consequence of Androcles's Choice
Pull the thorn from the lion's paw or not.		
Stay in the forest with the lion or leave to be on his own.		
Stand still when the lion rushes into the circus or try to run away.		

Review "Androcles and the Lion"

Theme in "Androcles and the Lion"

Answer the questions.

1. Androcles has a problem when he is alone in the forest. What is he afraid of?

    _____

2. Androcles chooses to help the lion. What does he do?

    _____

3. What is the consequence of Androcles's choice to help the lion?

    _____

4. Androcles has a solution to his problem. Why does he no longer feel afraid and alone?

    _____

5. What is the theme of this story?

    _____

    _____

    _____

Introduce "Pliny Saw It All" (B)

Know, Wonder, Learn

Complete the chart with what you know, wonder about, and learn from your reading.

Know	Wonder	Learn

Introduce "Pliny Saw It All" (B)

Draw Conclusions

Write a fact in each box. Then, write a conclusion you draw from the facts.

Fact from the Text	Fact from the Text	Fact from the Text

My Conclusion

These facts tell me that in ancient Pompeii

Introduce *Volcanoes!* (B)

Sequence Information

Complete the sentence in each box with information from the book about how a volcano works.

> ### How a Volcano Works

First, plates in the earth's crust

_____

↓

Then, the crust cracks and

_____

↓

Next, the magma becomes lava and either explodes or

_____

↓

ally, the volcano gets bigger from layers of

_____

Introduce *Volcanoes!* (A)

Answer Questions About a Text

Choose the answer.

1. How many years was Mount St. Helens "asleep" before it erupted?

   A. 15   **B.** 123   **C.** 80   **D.** 1,

2. How far did the ash cloud shoot into the sky?

   A. 15 miles   **C.** 80 miles

   B. 123 miles   **D.** 1,300 miles

3. What happens to people and animals if they get to much ash in their lungs?

   A. They fall asleep.   **C.** They canno

   B. They get sick.   **D.** They slow

4. What mixes to make the mudflow from Mount

   A. mud and fallen rock   **C.** melted

   B. fallen ash and cars   **D.** ash an

5. What happens to the top of the volcano af

   A. It is covered in fiery lava.

   B. The trees go back to normal.

   C. The volcano is 1,300 feet shorter.

   D. There are 57 new kinds of animals

Fin

LC 50

Introduce Volcanoes! (C)

Compare and Contrast

Write what is different about the two stories in the outer parts of the ovals. Write what is the same in the center where the ovals overlap.

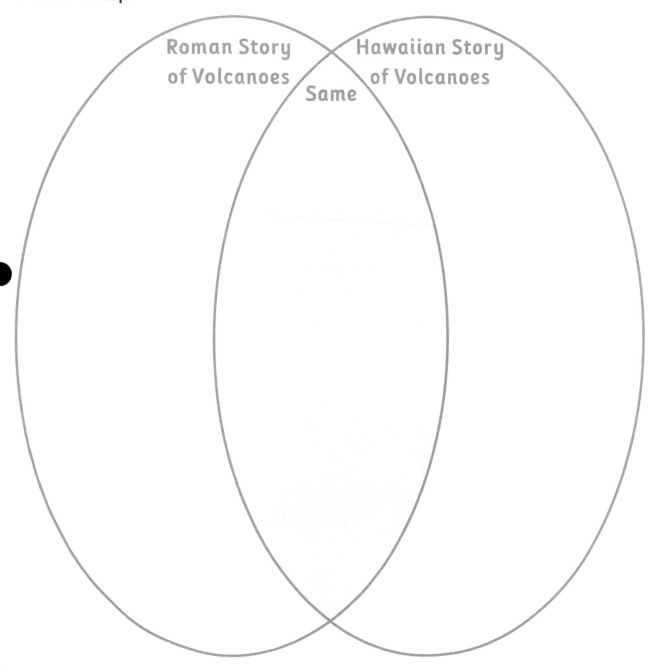

Roman Story of Volcanoes

Hawaiian Story of Volcanoes

Same

LITERATURE & COMPREHENSION

Review *Peter Pan*
Choices and Consequences

Write the choice the character makes. Then, write the consequence of the choice.

	Choice	Consequence
Page 87: Mrs. Darling says she will adopt Peter.	Peter says	Peter
Page 90: Peter is allowed to come back for Wendy every spring.	Peter forgets	Peter forgets
Page 92: Wendy becomes a mother. Peter comes back for her one more time.	Wendy decides	Wendy's

Reading Strategies Guide

Follow these strategies to make sure you understand what you read.

Before Reading

1. Do a Book Walk.
   - Look at the pictures.
   - Think about what kind of writing it is.
   - Look at the text parts, such as headings, captions, and special type.

2. Predict what you will read about.

During and After Reading

1. Stop and ask questions.
   - What just happened?
   - Did I learn anything new?
   - Can I describe what I just read?
   - What do I think will happen next?

2. When you don't understand something, repair your reading.
   - **Summarize:** Tell yourself in one or two sentences what just happened.
   - **Make inferences:** Use what you know to make guesses.
   - **Reread:** Read again a little more slowly, so you don't miss ideas.
   - **Read on:** If you have a question, read on to see if the answer is there.
   - **Use context clues:** Look for clues nearby to help you define new words.

Introduce *Clara and the Bookwagon*

Clara and the Bookwagon, Chapter 1

Choose the answer.

1. What are some of the things that Clara does on her family's farm?

    A. She helps cook and plant crops. She helps take care of animals and her siblings.

    B. She reads books to herself and to her siblings.

    C. She chops the wood for the cooking fire.

    D. She makes dinner by herself when her mother is doing other chores.

2. What does Clara want to do?

    A. learn to read

    B. plant seeds

    C. wash clothes

    D. go to school

3. What does Clara like to do?

    A. work on the farm

    B. care for her younger brother and sister

    C. listen to stories, dream, tell stories

    D. go to school with other children

4. How does Clara's mother feel about Clara's questions?

   A. She thinks Clara's questions are funny.

   B. She wants Clara to sit down so she can answer them.

   C. She thinks Clara is very smart and should go to school.

   D. She doesn't want to answer them because she's busy.

5. How does Clara's father feel about her dreaming?

   A. She should write about her dreams in a journal.

   B. She shouldn't dream because there isn't time.

   C. She should tell the family her dreams at dinner.

   D. She should dream because it is a good way to relax.

Explore *Clara and the Bookwagon,* Chapter 2
Compare and Contrast

Write what farm life is like in the top oval. Write what town life is like in the bottom oval. Write how the places are similar in the middle.

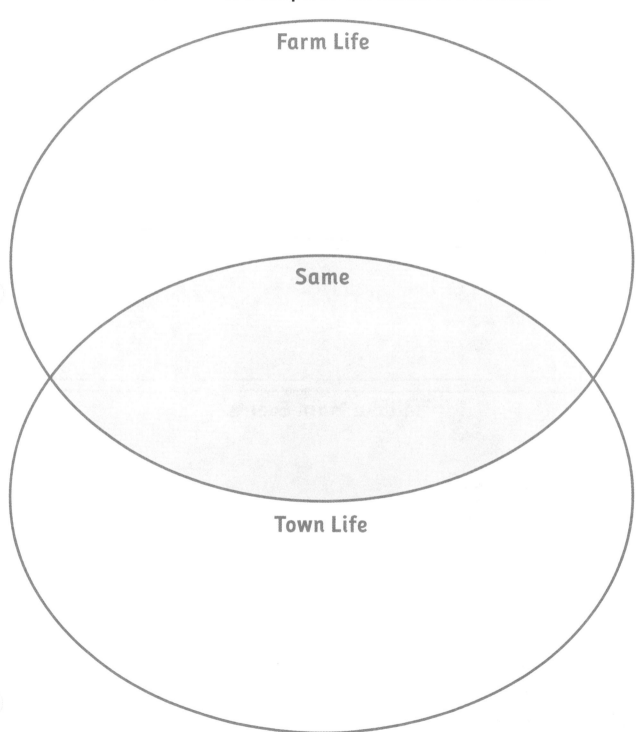

Farm Life

Same

Town Life

LITERATURE & COMPREHENSION

Explore *Clara and the Bookwagon,* Chapter 3 and 4

Sequence of Events

Fill in the boxes.

> **Title, Author, Characters, Setting**

> **Beginning Main Events**

> **Middle Main Events**

> **Ending Main Events**

Review *Clara and the Bookwagon*

Summarize the Story

Write a summary of *Clara and the Bookwagon*.

In the book *Clara and the Bookwagon* by Nancy Smiler Levinson,

a girl named Clara _____

_____

_____

_____

_____

_____

_____

_____

_____

LITERATURE & COMPREHENSION

Introduce "The Ugly Duckling"
"The Ugly Duckling"

Choose the answer.

1. How does the mother duck treat the ugly duckling?

   A. She takes care of him and defends him against the other animals.

   B. She makes fun of him and laughs at him like the other animals.

   C. She pretends that he is not one of her chicks and ignores him.

   D. She is mean to him and tries to bite him.

2. How do the other ducks and chickens in the farmyard treat the ugly duckling?

   A. They are nice to him.

   B. They bite him and laugh at him.

   C. They try to become his friends.

   D. They ignore him and pretend that he isn't there.

3. Why won't the cat and hen talk to the ugly duckling?

   A. They don't know how to talk to a duckling.

   B. They are afraid they will get in trouble.

   C. They think he cannot do anything important.

   D. The poor woman told them not to.

4. What does the ugly duckling become ?

   A. a duck

   B. a swan

   C. a goose

   D. a hen

5. What do the other swans and the children think of him ?

   A. He is beautiful.

   B. He is ugly.

   C. He is strange.

   D. He is old.

Explore "The Ugly Duckling"

Describe the Main Character

Describe the ugly duckling in the beginning, the middle, and the ending of the story. Support your answer with words from each part.

	My Description of the Ugly Duckling	Proof from the Story
Beginning		
Middle		
Ending		

Review "The Ugly Duckling"
The Moral and Me

Answer the questions. Then, draw a picture.

1. What is the moral of "The Ugly Duckling"?

   _____

   _____

   _____

2. Write about a time when you or someone you know learned this lesson.

   _____

   _____

   _____

3. Draw a picture that illustrates the time you wrote about in Exercise 2.

Explore "The Grasshopper and the Ant"
Cause and Effect

Write what the character does in the Cause box. Write how the character feels and what happens in the Effect box.

Cause	→	Effect

In summer, the grasshoper

In Scene 1, the grasshopper spends his time

In winter the grasshopper has

In summer, the ant

In Scene 1, the ant spends his time

In winter, the ant has

Review "The Grasshopper and the Ant"
The Moral and Me

Write the moral of the story. Draw a comic strip that shows how the moral happened to you.

The moral of the story is _____

_____

Explore "The Three Wishes"
Retell the Plot

Write the most important events from the story in sequence.

Beginning
A rabbit promises

First Event
The woodcutter's wife

Second Event
The woodcutter gets angry with his wife and

Final Event
The woodcutter wants to wish for all the gold in the world. Instead, he

Review "The Three Wishes"
The Moral of the Story

Write a summary of the story and answer the questions.

1. In this story, "The Three Wishes," _____

   _____

   _____

   _____

   _____

2. What does this story teach us? _____

   _____

   _____

   _____

3. I think this lesson is important because _____

   _____

Writing Skills

What Is a Sentence?
Sentences, Sentences

Guided Exercises

A **sentence** has two parts. The **naming part** tells whom or what the sentence is about. The **action part** tells what someone or something does.

  The cute dog wagged its tail.

- Does the example have both parts?
- Is it a complete thought?
- Underline the naming part of the sentence.
- Circle the action part of the sentence.

Add words to complete the thought.

1. My friend Andrew _____ .

2. His bike _____ .

3. The puppy _____ .

4. _____ ate a shiny apple.

What Is a Sentence?

Riddle Me

Read the words in each shape. Color each shape that has a complete sentence. Solve the riddle.

What kind of cup can't hold water?

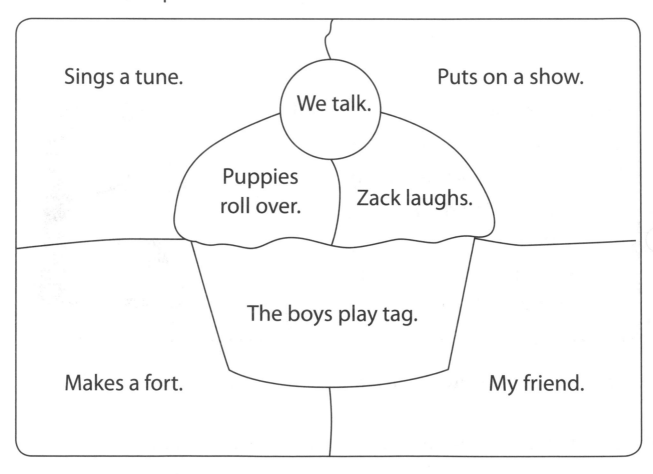

Sings a tune.

We talk.

Puts on a show.

Puppies roll over.

Zack laughs.

The boys play tag.

Makes a fort.

My friend.

Write your answer to the riddle.

_____

Sentence Beginnings and Endings
Begin and End It

Guided Exercises

> A sentence **begins** with a **capital letter**. It **ends** with an **end mark**. The end mark is often a **period**.

▶ ● **The green car won the race.**

▶ ● **Drivers put on helmets.**

- Are the examples complete sentences?
- Point to the capital letter at the beginning and the period at the end of each complete sentence.

▶ **came in last place.**

- Is this a complete sentence?
- Say words to make it a complete sentence.

Add a capital letter and period to the sentence.

1. _____ ert drove a silver car _____

2. _____ ars sped around the track _____

3. _____ he fans stood and cheered _____

Sentence Beginnings and Endings
Puddles of Sentences

Draw a smiley face beside the group of words that is a complete sentence. Write *X* next to the words that do not make a complete sentence.

1. Rain fell from the sky. _____

2. Lisa and I put on raincoats. _____

3. My rain boots. _____

Add a capital letter and period to the sentence.

4. _____ e jumped in the puddles _____

5. _____ ater splashed on us _____

6. _____ y boots got muddy and wet _____

Recognize and Fix Sentences
Is It Correct?

Guided Exercises

Sentences begin with **capital letters** and have **end marks**.

 Tyler runs in the park.

- Does this sentence start with a capital letter?
- Does this sentence end with an end mark?

 she laughed with her friend.

- Is this sentence correct?
- Fix the sentence.

Fix the sentence if it is not correct.

1. winter is a lot of fun.

2. My sister plays in the snow.

3. Diego made a snowman

4. our sled went down the hill

5. mom makes hot cocoa for us

Change the Sentence
Make Two into One

Change the pair of sentences into one sentence.

1. Cats play. Cats climb.

   _____

2. Dogs bark. Dogs run.

   _____

3. Flies buzz. Bees buzz.

   _____

4. Lions roar. Tigers roar.

   _____

5. Birds fly. Bugs fly.

   _____

WRITING SKILLS

Fix the Sentences
Revise It and Proofread It

When you look for errors in your writing and fix them, you are **proofreading**. When you change or rewrite to improve, you are **revising**.

▶ **joe likes rice. Joe likes potatoes**

- Proofread: ~~j~~Joe likes rice. Joe likes potatoes.
- Revised: Joe likes rice and potatoes.

Fix the sentence if it is missing a capital letter or end mark.

1. mena wants a board game

2. tina builds with blocks

Revise the sentences by combining the ones that are alike.

3. Alex played catch. Luka played catch.

_____

4. Lina likes cars. Lina likes trucks.

_____

Statements
State It

Guided Exercises

A **statement** is a telling sentence. It begins with a capital letter and ends with a period.

 Jessie drinks some milk.

- What does this sentence tell you?

 Lisa makes toast.

- What does this sentence tell you?
- These sentences are statements. Point to the first letter and end mark in each sentence.

Draw a line under the capital letter at the beginning of the statement. Circle the period at the end.

1. The dog eats the bone.

2. The spots are black.

3. The dog has four legs.

4. It is very playful.

Write your own statement about a dog.

5. _____

_____

Questions

Ask a Question

Write the correct end mark for the sentence.

1. Do you want to make a kite _____

2. Can Max find two wooden sticks _____

3. Why is the glue so sticky _____

4. Will you dip my brush in the paint _____

5. The wind will make the kite fly _____

Write *Q* if the sentence is a question. Write *X* if the sentence is not a question.

6. Did your kite crash? _____

7. I can fix the tail for you. _____

8. Will it fly now? _____

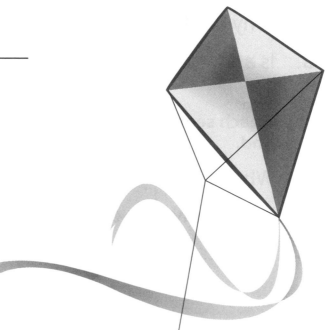

Exclamations and Commands
Bumblebee Buzz

Guided Exercises

An **exclamation** is a sentence that shows excitement or strong feelings. It ends with an exclamation mark.

A **command** is a sentence that gives an order or makes a request. It ends with a period.

▶ **A bee stung me!**

- How might you feel? Draw your face.
- The sentence is an exclamation.

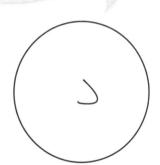

▶ **Put the bee down.**

- What does the sentence tell you to do? Circle the end mark.
- This sentence is a command.

Write an exclamation mark at the end of an exclamation.
Write a period at the end of a command.

1. Bees have so many eyes _____

2. Stay away from the hive _____

3. Look at the busy bee _____

4. That really hurt _____

Exclamations and Commands

Two Kinds of Sentences

Write a period at the end of each command.
Write an exclamation mark at the end of each exclamation.

1. The bike is going to crash _____

2. I am going to be late _____

3. Jump over the rope _____

4. Tony lost the house key _____

5. Put on your new raincoat _____

Match the two parts of the sentence. Then, write the complete sentence correctly.

6.
| take the dog | scare me |
| fireworks | for a walk |

7. _____

8. _____

Tell Me About It
Statements

Guided Exercises

A **statement** tells something.
It ends with a period.

 We can take a walk.

- What kind of sentence is this?
- Underline the statement. Circle the end mark.

 The sun is shining.

- What kind of sentence is this?
- Underline the statement. Circle the end mark.

Underline each sentence that makes a statement.

1. We will walk to the store.

2. Stop! Don't walk!

3. The light is red.

4. When will it turn green?

5. Now we can go.

Write your own statement about the picture.

6. _____

_____

Tell Me About It

Proofread the Sentences

Fix the statement. Add a capital letter and period.

1. _____ L ~~l~~uke plays with blocks _____ .

2. _____ fluffy chases her tail _____

3. _____ max chews a bone _____

Draw a picture and write your own statement about what is happening in it.

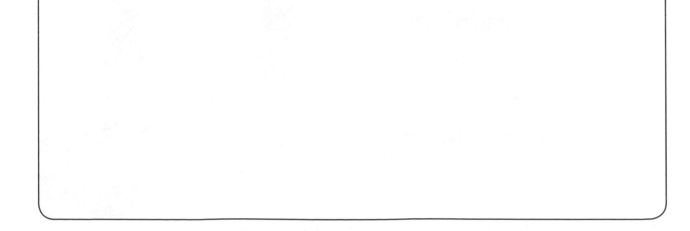

4. _____

_____

Ask Me About It
Questions, Questions

Guided Exercises

> A **question** asks something.
> It ends with a question mark.

 Are you hungry?

- Underline the question. Circle the end mark.

Underline each question.

1. What is Rosa eating?

2. It is flat and round.

3. Does it have red sauce?

Add an asking word to make a question about the picture. Use a capital letter to begin and a question mark to end the sentence.

> who   does   how   what

4. _____ is eating spaghetti ____

5. _____ is on top ____

6. _____ it smell good ____

7. _____ does it taste ____

Ask Me About It

Proofread Questions

Fix the question. Add a capital letter and question mark.

1. who is going _____

2. what will you do _____

3. did you have fun _____

4. can you show me _____

5. are you sleepy _____

Write your own question.

6. _____

_____

Shout About It
Exclamations and Commands

Guided Exercises

An **exclamation** shows excitement. It ends with an exclamation mark. A **command** is an order or a request. It ends with a period.

 You're the winner!
- What kind of sentence is this?

 Give her the prize.
- What kind of sentence is this?

Choose an exclamation or command to answer the question.

Get me crayons, please.   I do!

I'm here!   Go to bed now.

1. Who wants to go? _____

2. Where's Luke? _____

3. I'm sleepy. What should I do? _____

4. What do you need? _____

Shout About It
A Box for Chen

Add an exclamation mark or period to the end of the sentence.

1. The gift is here _____

2. Chen could not wait _____

3. Put the box down _____

4. Don't open it _____

5. Wait for the party _____

6. Chen was so happy _____

 Reward ....

Draw a picture of what is inside Chen's box.
Write an exclamation to go with your picture.

Revise Sentences

End Mark Cards

Cut out each card. Use the cards to punctuate sentences.

.	?	!
.	?	!
.	?	!
.	?	!

WRITING SKILLS

Revise Sentences
Change the Type of Sentence

Guided Exercises

The four kinds of sentences are **statements**, **questions**, **exclamations**, and **commands**.

▶ **Are you home? You are home.**

- Circle the statement and underline the question.

▶ **They are here! Say hello.**

- Circle the exclamation and underline the command.

Change the sentence to an exclamation.

1. Do I love you? _____

Change the sentence to a command.

2. Will you walk the dog? _____

Change the sentence to a statement.

3. Can she read? _____

Change the sentence to a question.

4. It is late. _____

Revise Sentences
End Mark Game

Place an end mark at the end of the sentence.

You are late	Did you call	This is fun
Come here	Can we go	Are you home
You look nice	Go now	We're going to the park
May we stay	I feel great	Sit down

Write Different Types of Sentences

Write About a Picture

Write four sentences about the picture. Write a statement, a question, an exclamation, and a command.

_____

_____

_____

_____

_____

_____

_____

_____

WRITING SKILLS

WRITING SKILLS

What Is a Noun?

Jungle of Nouns

Guided Exercises

> A **noun** names a person, place, or thing.

Billy stops and listens.

- Who stops? Underline the noun that names the person.

Serena runs to the cave.

- What does Serena run to? Underline the noun that names the place.

A lion roars.

- What roars? Underline the noun that names the thing.

Color only the boxes that contain nouns. Color nouns for people blue. Color nouns for places yellow. Color nouns for things green.

hiker	Africa	vines
dark	tent	Monday
jungle	bugs	muddy

What Is a Noun?

Noun Safari

Circle the nouns in the sentence.

1. The jeep goes down a path.

2. The jungle is in Africa.

3. Monkeys and birds hide in the trees.

4. Lisa takes a picture.

5. On Friday, the visitors go home.

6. The animals sleep.

Reward ....

WRITING SKILLS

Common and Proper Nouns
Special Nouns

WRITING SKILLS

Guided Exercises

A **common noun** names any person, place, or thing. It begins with a small letter.
A **proper noun** names a special person, place, or thing. It begins with a capital letter.

▶ **My friend went on a trip.**

- Which word names any person?
- This word is a **common noun**. Circle the first letter. Is it a big or a small letter?

▶ **Sue left on Friday.**

- Which word names a special person?
- This word is a **proper noun**. Circle the first letter. Is it a big or a small letter?

Match the common nouns with the proper nouns.

1.

friend	Fluffy
cat	August
month	Bob

Write a proper noun for the common noun.

2. team _____   3. city_____

Common and Proper Nouns

Puzzled About Nouns

Match the common nouns with the proper nouns.

1.

day	July
zoo	Monday
girl	City Zoo
month	Fran

Circle the proper nouns. Underline the common nouns.

2. Billy and Jess ride a bus.

3. The cars stop on Pine Street.

4. Saturday is soccer day.

5. Our team plays the Bulls.

Write one sentence about where you live. Use at least one common noun and one proper noun.

6. _____

_____

WRITING SKILLS

Step-by-Step
Follow Steps in Order

Steps tell what you need to do to complete a task or reach a goal.

How to Make Toast

Step 1 Put bread in toaster.

Step 2 Press the button and wait for bread to pop up.

Step 3 Put bread on plate.

Step 4 Spread butter on top.

- Which step do you do first? Circle it.
- Which step do you do *after* you put the bread on the plate? Underline it.

Match the steps to the correct order for how to do a jigsaw puzzle.

Fit more pieces together until the puzzle is complete.   Step 1

Connect the shapes that fit together.   Step 2

Take all the puzzle pieces out of the box.   Step 3

Step-by-Step
Follow the Steps

Follow these steps to make a house from a square of paper.

Step 1   Fold a square of paper in half. Then, unfold it.

Step 2   Fold in the two top corners to the center.

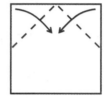

Step 3   Fold the tip of one corner up. The point should stick above the top of the paper.

Step 4   Fold in the side edges of the paper.

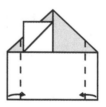

Step 5   Turn the paper over. Add windows and a door to the house.

Details Count
Use Details

Steps need **details** to create a clear picture of what to do.

 First, put on your socks. Next, put on your right sneaker. Last, go and play!

- Read the steps. What detail is missing?

 It's bedtime. First, put on your pajamas. Last, turn out the light.

- Read the steps. What detail is missing?

Follow the steps to draw a square. Then, fill in the missing step to complete the shape.

First, draw a line from A to B.

Then, draw a line from B to C.

Next, draw a line from D to C.

Finally, _____.

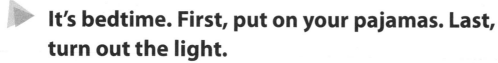

A.   B.

D.   C.

Details Count
Include All the Details

These pictures show how to plant a seed. Write the steps for planting a seed. Don't miss any details in your steps.

1. _____

2. _____

3. _____

4. _____

5. Add a step that you think is missing.

_____

_____

Follow Steps
Fix the Order

Guided Exercises

Steps must be followed in order.
Steps cannot be skipped.

 Bake the apple pie at 350 degrees. Slice the apples. Put the sliced apples in the unbaked pie shell. Serve the pie warm.

- Which step is not in order? Underline it. This step is not in order because it should not be done first.
- Which step could be added?

Read the steps to run a bubble bath. Circle the step that is in the wrong order. Add the missing step.

Put the stopper in the tub.

Hop in and enjoy the bubbles.

Add bubble bath liquid or powder.

_____

Let the tub fill.

Turn off the water.

Follow Steps

Think of a Process

What do you know how to do that requires steps or directions that must be followed in order? What do you know how to make or build? Brainstorm ideas for processes that use steps.

_____

_____

_____

_____

_____

_____

_____

_____

_____

WRITING SKILLS

Organize Ideas

Review Steps in a Process

Look carefully at the drawing. Think of the steps needed to draw this robot.

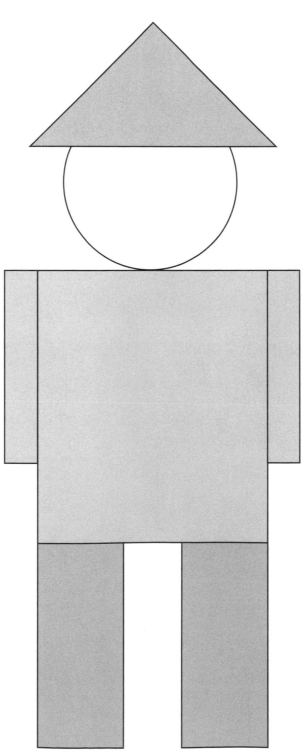

Organize Ideas
Fill In Your Steps

Write a title that tells what your steps are about. Then write the four most important steps in the boxes in the graphic organizer, in order. You do not have to use complete sentences.

How to

Organize Ideas

How to Use a Graphic Organizer

Guided Exercises

A **graphic organizer** helps organize ideas before you begin writing. Some graphic organizers show how steps or ideas are connected in order.

 There are four steps to drawing a robot.

- Look at the drawing and think of the steps needed to draw a robot.

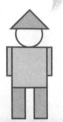

Complete the graphic organizer so it shows the steps for drawing a robot. Look at the drawing for ideas. You do not have to write in complete sentences.

> Draw a circle.

↓

> Draw a rectangle underneath.

↓

>

↓

>

Write Steps Using a Graphic Organizer

Write the Steps

Enter the title for your how-to steps. Write at least four detailed steps in the correct order. Use numbers to help readers follow your steps.

> How to _____

_____

_____

_____

_____

_____

_____

_____

WRITING SKILLS

What Is a Verb?
Herb's Verbs

Guided Exercises

A **verb** is a word that shows action.

 Herb dances in the barnyard.

- What does Herb do? Underline the word that tells what Herb does. This word is an action word or **verb**. It tells us what Herb is doing.

 He claps and stomps, too.

- Underline two more verbs that tell what Herb does.

Underline the verb or verbs in the sentence.

1. Molly stirs the soup.

2. Meg and Bill build a tower.

3. Squirrels climb trees and eat nuts.

4. Bo reads a story to his brother.

5. Jay and Rick kick and chase the ball.

6. Maria jumps high and catches it.

What Is a Verb?

Fiddle-Dee-Dee Verbs

Underline the verb or verbs in the sentence.

1. The farmer plays a fiddle.

2. The big orange roosters crow.

3. Mrs. Hen and her chick flap their wings.

4. Some of the pigs laugh.

5. Old Grey Donkey turns his head and runs.

6. The clock strikes nine.

7. Everyone goes home.

Reward ....

Action Verbs
Interesting Verbs

Guided Exercises

Use interesting verbs to tell more about the action.

 A snake goes into the grass.
A snake slithers into the grass.

- In the second sentence, which word means about the same thing as *goes*? Circle it. This word is a more interesting verb.

Write a more interesting verb for the underlined verb. Use the verbs in the word bank.

> gobbles   howls   gallops   paints

1. Molly <u>makes</u> a picture. _____

2. The horse <u>runs</u> to the gate. _____

3. A flock of birds <u>eats</u> the seeds. _____

4. The wind <u>blows</u>. _____

Action Verbs
Verb Crossword

Find a more interesting verb for the underlined word. Write the verb in the crossword. Use the verbs in the word bank.

    wade   boil   whisper   snooze   gulp   sprout

1. Trees <u>grow</u> new leaves.
2. Nicky and Sue <u>tell</u> a secret.
3. The Cub Scouts <u>cook</u> hotdogs.
4. Let's <u>step</u> in the pond.
5. Bats <u>sleep</u> all day.
6. The thirsty boys <u>drink</u> milk.

Other Verbs
Verb Play

Guided Exercises

These special verbs do not show action.

am   is   are   was   were

 Meg, Lisa, and Ryan are the pigs in the play.

- Underline the verb. This verb does not show action.

 José is the wolf in the play.

- Underline the verb. This verb does not show action.

Find the character. Use a brown pencil or crayon to color each space that has a verb that does **not** show action.

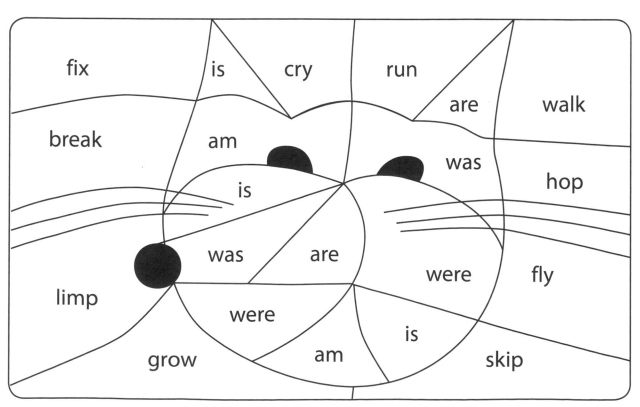

Other Verbs

Am, Is, Are, Was, Were

Circle the verb in the sentence.

1. The wolf was in the woods.

2. The three pigs are brothers.

3. The play is today.

4. I am the greeter.

Write two sentences about the pigs or the wolf. Use verbs that do not show action.

5. _____

   _____

6. _____

   _____

Beginning, Middle, and End
Sequencing

Guided Exercises

> A **sequence** is the order in which things happen. A sequence has a beginning, a middle, and an end.

 _____ **I went food shopping in the morning.** _____ **Later,**

I did chores around my house. _____ **Finally, I cooked**

dinner.

- Write 1 for the beginning of the sequence.
- Write 2 for the middle of the sequence.
- Write 3 for the end of the sequence and underline it.

Read the story. Then, write the beginning, middle, and end.

> Once upon a time in a kingdom far away, a prince met a princess. They danced together. They lived happily ever after.

Beginning _____

Middle _____

End _____

Beginning, Middle, and End
How to Grow a Plant

Put the sequence in the correct order: beginning, middle, and end.

> The plants grew very tall.
>
> We put seeds in a pot with soil.
>
> The seeds got sun and water.

Beginning _____

Middle _____

End _____

Reward. . . . .

Draw a picture that shows the end of the sequence.

Use Order Words

Order Words

WRITING SKILLS

Guided Exercises

> Order words help organize a series of steps or a story, showing the beginning, middle, and end.

Going to the Movies

 _____, buy a ticket. _____, find a seat.

_____, watch the movie.

- What happens in the beginning? Label it *First*.
- What happens in the middle? Label it *Next*.
- What happens in the end? Label it *Finally*.

Put the sequence in the correct order: beginning, middle, and end.

> We ate the pie after dinner.
> Grandma picked cherries.
> She baked a cherry pie.

First _____

Next _____

Finally _____

What Happens Next?

Put It in Order

Read the story. Add order words so that the story makes sense. Use the order words in the word bank. The words *Next* and *Then* can be used more than once.

> First   Next   Then   Later   At last   Finally

It was moving day. _____ , Mom packed the boxes.

_____ , Dad carried boxes. _____ ,

Shah carried boxes. _____ , Neela carried boxes.

_____ , no boxes were left. _____ , all boxes

were on the truck.

Organize Ideas
Use a Graphic Organizer

Guided Exercises

A **step-by-step graphic organizer** can show a sequence of events in the order in which they occurred.

▶ **Beth served cake. Beth greeted her guests. Beth opened the presents. Beth sent the invitations. Beth decorated the room.**

- These events happened during Beth's birthday party. Use the graphic organizer to put them in order.
- Circle the event that comes first in this sequence.

Write the events in the boxes in the order they happened.

```
┌─────────────────────────────────────┐
│                                     │
└─────────────────────────────────────┘
                 ↓
┌─────────────────────────────────────┐
│                                     │
└─────────────────────────────────────┘
                 ↓
┌─────────────────────────────────────┐
│                                     │
└─────────────────────────────────────┘
                 ↓
┌─────────────────────────────────────┐
│                                     │
└─────────────────────────────────────┘
                 ↓
┌─────────────────────────────────────┐
│                                     │
└─────────────────────────────────────┘
```

Organize Ideas

Complete a Graphic Organizer

Write the name of the topic you chose. Then, write four events in the boxes. Keep the events in the order in which they happened. You do not have to write complete sentences.

Topic:

Write a Sequence

Write Your Sequence

Write a sequence of events about a topic. Write a title, and then write steps in complete sentences. Begin each sentence with an order word.

Title:

Capital Letters in the Heading of a Letter

A Letter to Aunt Janie

Use Ernesto's letter to Aunt Janie as you work through the lessons in the unit.

213 Wild Oak Drive
Portland, Maine 04101
June 15, 2010

Dear Aunt Janie,
    I miss you! Please come visit us again.

Hugs and kisses,
Ernesto

Capital Letters in the Heading of a Letter

Fix the Headings

Correct the mistakes in the heading. Cross out the incorrect letter and write the correct letter above.

1. 2111 tubb Street

   Elk city, Kansas 67344

   april 25, 2000

2. 77 Dole drive

   troy, New york 12180

   may 17, 2008

Complete the heading.

3. 432 ___umpy ___oad

   ___lano, ___exas 75075

   ___anuary 2, 2011

Commas in the Heading of a Letter

Commas in Headings

Guided Exercises

In a heading, use a **comma** between the city and the state. Use a **comma** between the day and the year, too.

213 Wild Oak Drive
Portland, Maine 04101
June 15, 2010

- Underline the city. Underline the state.
- Circle the comma between the city and the state.
- Underline the day. Underline the year.
- Circle the comma between the day and the year.

Circle the commas. Use the words in the word bank to write what comes next in each heading.

2009	Georgia

1. Atlanta, _____

2. May 2, _____

Texas	2000

3. Houston, _____

4. July 19, _____

WRITING SKILLS

Commas in the Heading of a Letter
Commas, Please

Look at the headings for four different letters. Write commas where needed.

1.
> 11 Palm Tree Drive
> Ocala Florida 34474
> June 22 2011

3.
> 40 Elm Street
> Dallas Texas 75205
> April 17 2005

2.
> 9555 Orange Avenue
> Park City Kansas 67204
> December 31 2009

4.
> 261 Lemon Lane
> Zuni New Mexico 87327
> October 1 2010

Connect the dots to spell the name of the state in box 1. Color the space inside the lines to see a mark used to separate parts of an address or a date.

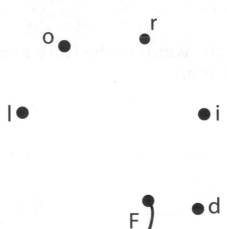
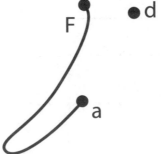

Greeting and Closing of a Letter
Capital Letters and Commas in Letters

Guided Exercises

A **greeting** begins with a capital letter and ends with a comma. The **closing** begins with a capital letter and ends with a comma, too.

 Dear Aunt Janie,

- This is the letter's greeting. Underline the first capital letter. Circle the end mark.

 Hugs and kisses,

- This is the closing. Underline the capital letter. Circle the end mark.

Underline the greetings and closings that are written correctly. Fix those that are incorrect.

1. Your friend,

2. Thank you,

3. Write soon

4. Hi Hank,

5. Love,

6. dear Sammy

WRITING SKILLS

Greeting and Closing of a Letter

Letter Fixes

Fix the greetings and the closings. Put a line through each mistake. Write the correct letter or end mark above the mistake. The first one has been done for you.

1. Dear Mr. Jones,

2. hi Adam,

3. dear Mimi,

4. hello Dr. Evans.

5. Write soon.

6. Love!

7. your friend,

8. Goodbye.

9. Thank you

10. your cousin,

What Is a Friendly Letter?
Letter from Rico

WRITING SKILLS

Use the letter from Rico as you work through the lessons in the unit.

20 Leo Street
Butler, TN 37640
December 12, 2011

Dear Jamal,

    I had a great time in Denver with my family. We went to visit my grandparents.

    First, we went to Pike's Peak. We took a train to get there. The train went high up in the mountains. The next day, we saw more of the Rocky Mountains. We went to Red Rock. Guess what color the rocks are? The last day, we went to the science museum and the zoo.

    I hope your trip was fun like mine was.

Your friend,
Rico

What Is a Friendly Letter?

To Whom Are You Writing?

Gina is writing friendly letters. Read the sentence from each letter, and circle the correct audience.

1. Please come to my birthday party.

   A. Dr. James

   B. her friend Emily

2. I hope you and Grandpa are well.

   A. Grandma

   B. her brother Ed

3. We are coming for a visit in April.

   A. Aunt Flo

   B. her neighbor

4. I miss playing with you since you moved.

   A. Mom

   B. her friend Jason

5. I had fun playing in the park with you.

   A. Mayor Lee

   B. Cousin Jane

Friendly Letter Format
The Form of a Friendly Letter

Guided Exercises

A friendly letter has five parts: the **heading**, **greeting**, **body**, **closing**, and **signature**.

 Use the Letter from Rico to answer the questions.

- Which part includes the date?
- Which part shows who is receiving the letter?
- Which part has the message?
- Which part shows how the letter ends?
- Which part shows who wrote the letter?

Write the name of each part of the letter.

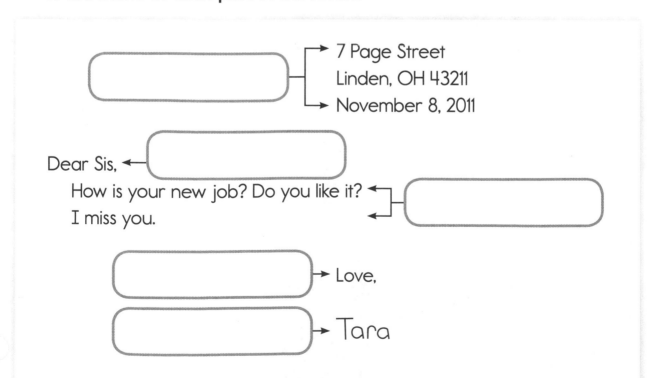

7 Page Street
Linden, OH 43211
November 8, 2011

Dear Sis,
    How is your new job? Do you like it?
    I miss you.

Love,

Tara

Friendly Letter Format

Fill In the Information

Pretend you are writing this letter to your friend. Add the missing information.

_____

_____

_____

_____ ,

I just read some great books. They were about this woman named Amelia Bedelia. She is so funny!

I think you would like these books, too.

_____ ,

_____

Organize a Letter
Organize the Body of a Letter

The body of a letter starts with a **beginning sentence** and ends with a **concluding sentence**. Details are often in **time order**.

▶ **Use the Letter from Rico to complete the graphic organizer.**

Beginning Sentence
I had a great time in Denver with my family.

Detail

Detail

Detail
Rocky Mountains, Red Rock

Concluding Sentence
I hope your trip was fun like mine was.

Organize a Letter
Use a Graphic Organizer

Use the graphic organizer to help you plan the body of your own friendly letter. You do not have to write complete sentences for the details.

Beginning Sentence

Detail

Detail

Detail

Concluding Sentence

Address an Envelope
How to Address an Envelope

WRITING SKILLS

Guided Exercises

A letter is placed in an **envelope** before it can be mailed. The envelope needs a name, a **delivery address**, a **return address**, and a **stamp**.

Mr. James Small
50 Shore Drive
New City, IL 62563

Mrs. Lynn Viera
64 Wells Ave.
Tulsa, OK 74101

- Circle the name of the person sending the letter. This is part of the **return address**.
- Underline the name of the person receiving the letter. This is part of the **delivery address**.
- Where is the stamp? Circle it. All mail needs a **stamp**.

Write the following information in the correct places on a real envelope.

1. **To**: Ms. Sally Storm
   11 Wills Ave.
   Rutland, VT 05701

2. **From**: Mr. Dan Denton
   74 Handy Street
   New York, NY 10036

3. Draw a stamp where the stamp should be.

Address an Envelope

Address Your Envelope

Use the space below to practice addressing your envelope. When you are ready, address a real envelope with your own home address and the address of the person to whom you are writing your letter.

Write a Friendly Letter

Write to Someone You Know

Write a friendly letter.

LANGUAGE ARTS ORANGE

Write a Friendly Letter
Tell Me About My Friendly Letter

Have another person read your friendly letter and answer the questions.

1. What is the purpose of the letter? Does the letter share news, feelings, or thoughts?

   _____

   _____

2. Who is the audience for this letter? Are the greeting and closing appropriate?

   _____

   _____

3. Are the ideas written in an order that makes sense?

   _____

4. Is there a beginning sentence that introduces the main idea of the letter? What is it?

   _____

5. Is there a concluding sentence that summarizes the reason for writing the letter? What is it?

   _____

6. Does the letter have a beginning, middle, and end? If not, which is missing?

_____

7. What are some transition words the writer uses to help connect the ideas?

_____

8. Is the letter clear? How could the writing be improved?

_____

_____

One or Many?
One and More Than One

Guided Exercises

> A **singular noun** names one. A **plural noun** names more than one. Add –*s* or –*es* to make a noun plural.

 I see a dump truck, three cars, and two buses.

- Underline the nouns.
- Draw a circle around the –*s* or the –*es* at the end of each plural noun. Why was –*es* added to *bus* to make it plural?

Write the plural form of the noun. Add –*s* or –*es* to the end.

1. pond _____

2. box _____

3. wish _____

4. clip _____

Write a sentence that uses the plural of *batch*.

5. _____

_____

_____

One or Many?

A Lot of Nouns

Write the missing nouns.

	Singular	Plural
1.	jar	
2.	brush	
3.		foxes
4.	bucket	
5.	snake	
6.	dress	
7.		tents
8.		camels

Choose a plural noun from the chart. Use the noun in a sentence.

9. _____

_____

More Plural Nouns
Tricky Nouns

Guided Exercises

Some plural nouns have special spellings.

 I lost one tooth. He lost two teeth.

- Underline the singular noun. Circle the plural noun. The plural noun is formed by changing the middle letters.

 The cat chased one white mouse and two brown mice.

- Underline the singular noun. Circle the plural noun. The plural noun is formed by changing the entire word.

Use the correct singular or plural form of the underlined noun to complete the sentence.

1. I saw one <u>woman</u>, and two more _____ were waiting.

2. There was one <u>goose</u> in the garden, and there were three

   _____ by the lake.

3. Two <u>children</u> were playing ball, and one _____ was watching.

More Plural Nouns

Goose and Geese

Choose the correct word. Write it in the space.

1. childs   children   two _____

2. mice   mouses   four _____

3. gooses   geese   some _____

4. man   men   one _____

5. feet   foots   many _____

Write a sentence that uses the plural of *tooth*.

6. _____

_____

_____

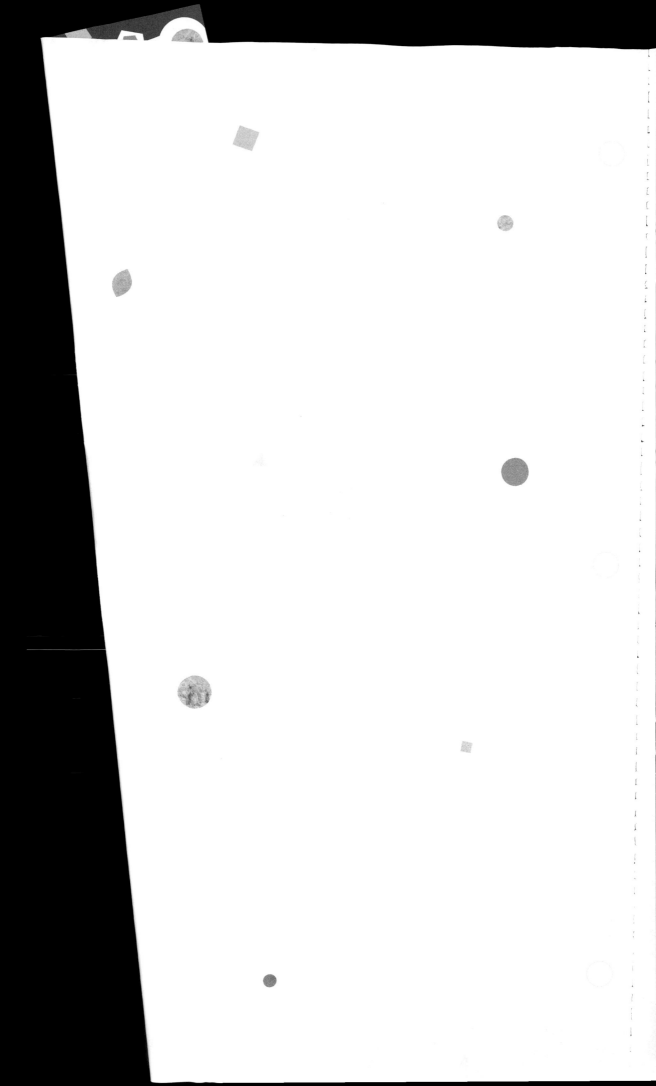

What Is a Thank-You Note

Jessica's Thank-You Note

**Use Jessica's thank-you note as you wor
in the unit.**

Dear Aunt Mary,
    Thank you for the bec
    The blanket has the s
has the same pink and
when I touch it. It is so
    I will think of you e

What Is a Thank-You Note?

The Purpose of a Thank-You Note

Guided Exercises

The purpose of a **thank-you note** is to thank someone. The person to whom the note is written is the **audience**.

 Look at Jessica's Thank-You Note.

- Why did Jessica write this note? Point to the sentence that tells why she wrote it. This is the **purpose** of the thank-you note.

- Who is the audience for the thank-you note? Point to the name.

Circle *friendly letter* or *thank-you note* to show which one you should write for the example.

1. You get a gift.

    A. friendly letter   **B.** thank-you note

2. You want to share some news.

    A. friendly letter   **B.** thank-you note

3. You want to ask how someone feels.

    A. friendly letter   **B.** thank-you note

4. Your neighbor helped you.

    A. friendly letter   **B.** thank-you note

What Is a Thank-You Note?

Friendly Letters and Thank-You Notes

What kind of writing is it? Write *friendly letter* or *thank-you note* after the example.

1. Thank you for baking the cookies.

   _____

2. How are you and Grandpa?

   _____

3. I had fun when I stayed at your house.

   _____

4. We just got back from our camping trip.

   _____

5. You were so helpful during the yard sale.

   _____

Use the Friendly Letter Format
Parts of a Thank-You Note

Guided Exercises

A thank-you note has five parts: the **heading**, **greeting**, **body**, **closing**, and **signature**.

 Look at the parts of Jessica's Thank-You Note.

- Which part of Jessica's Thank-You Note contains the address?
- Which part of the note says "Dear Aunt Mary"?

Answer the riddle to name the part of Jessica's Thank-You Note.

1. My name is Jessica. I wrote this thank-you note. In which part of the note did I write my name? _____

2. I describe the blanket Aunt Mary made. What part of the note am I? _____

3. I'm a word that shows how much Jessica cares about her aunt. I am followed by a comma. What part of the note am I? _____

4. I am the date the letter was written. In which part of the note am I? _____

5. I call the blanket beautiful. What part of the note am I? _____

Use the Friendly Letter Format

Format a Thank-You Note

Write each part of the thank-you note on the line where it belongs.

Your cousin,   January 9, 2011   Dear Ray,

22 Rose Street   Mike   Rock Hill, UT 29730

Thank you for taking me to the zoo. I had a great time.

_____

_____

_____

_____

_____

_____

_____

_____

Thank-You Note Plan
Main Idea and Details

Guided Exercises

The body of a thank-you note includes a **main idea** and **supporting details**. It also states the writer's **opinion** or feelings.

 Jessica used the graphic organizer below to write her thank-you note.

- Point to the sentence that tells you why Jessica wrote the note. This is the **main idea**.
- Point to the first reason why Jessica loves the blanket. This is a **supporting detail**.

Use Jessica's Thank-You Note to fill in the other details on the graphic organizer.

Main Idea
thank Aunt Mary for the blanket

Supporting Detail
same colors as my room

Supporting Detail

Supporting Detail

Thank-You Note Plan

Thank-You Note Graphic Organizer

Use the graphic organizer to plan the body of your own thank-you note. Write your main idea and three supporting details.

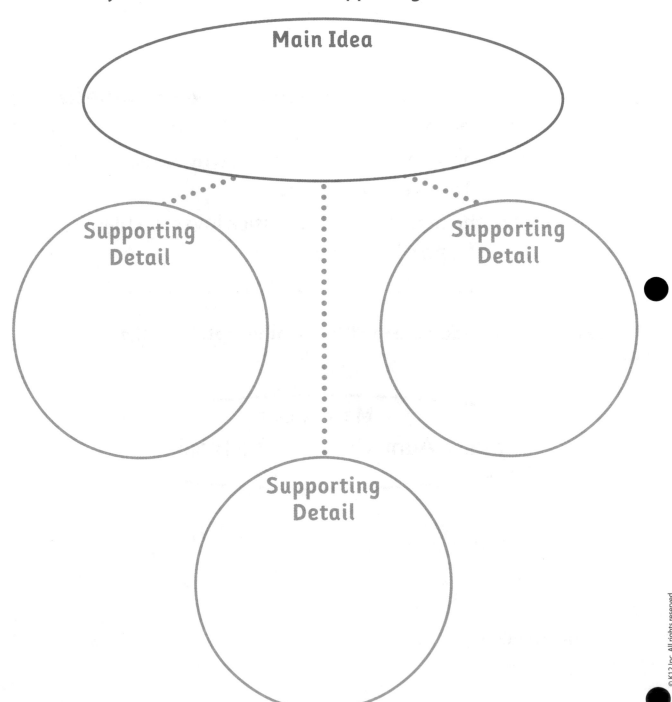

Main Idea

Supporting Detail

Supporting Detail

Supporting Detail

Send a Thank-You Note
How to Use E-mail to Send a Thank-You Note

WRITING SKILLS

Guided Exercises

An **e-mail** is a letter or note that is sent online from your computer. The body of an e-mail is the same as the body of a letter or a thank-you note.

▶ **An e-mail follows a form.**

	To:	Terry@email.com
Send	From:	Bree@email.com
	Subject:	Thank you for the gift!

- Where do you type the **e-mail** address of the person receiving the e-mail? Circle it. This is the **To** line.

- Where do you write what the e-mail is about? Underline it. This is the **Subject** line.

- How do you send the e-mail? Draw an X on the button you click.

Pia wants to send an e-mail thank-you note to Jake. Write *Jake, Pia,* and a subject on the correct lines in the e-mail form.

	To:	_____ @email.com
Send	From:	_____ @email.com
	Subject:	_____

Send a Thank-You Note
Address an Envelope and an E-mail

Address this envelope.

1. Write your real return address.

2. Write the address of the person to whom you are writing your thank-you note.

Fill in the e-mail form.

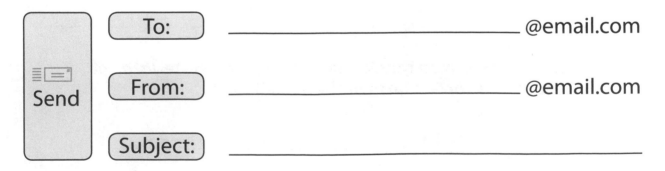

	To:	_____ @email.com
Send	From:	_____ @email.com
	Subject:	_____

3. Complete the e-mail form with the name of the person you are thanking and a subject for your thank-you note.

Write a Thank-You Note

Write to Say Thank You

Write your thank-you note.

_____

_____

_____

_____

_____

_____

_____

_____

_____

_____

WRITING SKILLS

_____

_____

_____

_____

_____

_____

_____

_____

_____

_____

Write a Thank-You Note

Tell Me About My Thank-You Note

Have another person read your thank-you note and answer these questions.

1. What is the purpose of the thank-you note?

   _____

   _____

2. Who is the audience for this note?

   _____

3. Are the greeting and closing appropriate for the audience? Why or why not?

   _____

4. What is the main idea?

   _____

5. Are there details to support the main idea? Name one.

   _____

6. Is there a beginning sentence that introduces the main idea of the note?

   _____

7. Is there a concluding sentence that summarizes the reason for writing the note?

_____

8. Does the writer express an opinion in the note?

_____

9. Is there anything the writer could do to make the note even stronger? If so, explain what the writer could do.

_____

_____

_____

Nouns and Verbs
Subjects and Verbs

Guided Exercises

Every sentence has a naming part, or **subject**, and an action part, or **verb**.

▶  **A skunk sat.**
  - The **subject** is circled; it tells *who*.
  - The **verb** is underlined; it tells *what* the subject does.

▶ **The skunk stunk.**
  - Circle the subject.
  - Underline the verb.

Circle the subject. Underline the verb.

1. Jack fishes.

2. Our dog barks.

3. The gardener works.

4. Meg and Jeff dance.

Nouns and Verbs
Names and Actions

Read the subject in the sentence. Choose the best verb from the word bank to complete the sentence.

| purr | swim | fly | moo |

1. Red birds _____.

2. Kittens _____.

3. Sharks _____.

4. Cows _____.

Circle the subject in the sentence.

5. My friends love camping.

6. Emma goes on a hike.

7. Max grills hotdogs.

8. The owls hoot.

Singular Nouns and Verbs
Make Subjects and Verbs Agree

WRITING SKILLS

Guided Exercises

Subjects and verbs must fit together. To make most verbs **agree** with singular subjects, add *s* to the end of the verb.

 The cow **moos.**

- Point to the verb. Circle the *s* at the end.
- Do the subject and verb agree?

 The chick **peep.**

- Point to the verb. Is it correct?
- Add *s* to the end. Now the subject and verb agree.

Match the subject and verb that fit together.

1. My toy

      spin.

      spins.

2. 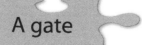 A gate

      opens.

      open.

Singular Nouns and Verbs
I Agree!

Choose the best word from the word bank to complete the sentence.

| plays | climbs | sleep | sets | rise |

1. Jay _____ to the tree house.

2. He _____ with his friend.

3. The sun _____ behind the trees.

Write a complete sentence about a tree house. Use a singular subject and a singular verb.

4. _____

_____

_____

_____

_____

Plural Nouns and Verbs
Plural Subjects and Verbs

Guided Exercises

Subjects and verbs must fit together. A plural noun uses a verb that does not have an *s* at the end.

 The cows **moo.**

- Point to the *s* at the end of the plural subject. Circle the verb.
- Do the subject and verb agree?

 Two chick **peep.**

- Point to the subject. Is it correct?
- Add an *s* to the subject to make it fit with the verb.

Match the subject and verb that fit together.

1. The trees

grow.

grows.

2. Some eggs

cracks.

crack.

Plural Nouns and Verbs

Plural Match Up

Underline the correct verb in the sentence.

1. The girls (draw,   draws).

2. Two doors (open,   opens).

3. These cubs (climbs,   climb).

4. Some slides (dip,   dips).

5. Their hands (clap,   clap).

6. Our noses (wiggle,   wiggles).

7. The ovens (bake,   bakes).

8. The birds (flaps,   flap) their wings.

9. Two sunflowers (grow,   grows) tall.

Write a verb to complete the sentence.

10. The bees _____.

What Is a Paragraph?
Winnie's Paragraph

Use Winnie's paragraph as you work through the lessons in the unit.

There are many kinds of animal homes. Animals live in trees or inside caves. Other animals live below the ground. Some animals live in water. They can even live under the snow. A snail's home is its shell. It carries the shell around on its back. Animal homes are not all the same.

WRITING SKILLS

What Is a Paragraph?
Sentences That Go Together

Guided Exercises

A **paragraph** is a group of sentences all about one topic. The **topic** is the subject of the paragraph.

 The topic of Winnie's Paragraph is animal homes.

- Look at the paragraph and find some things that tell you about animal homes.
- How do you know it is a paragraph?

Read the paragraph and answer the questions.

> It is fun to plant seeds and watch them grow. My sister likes flowers. First, choose the seeds you want to plant. You can plant vegetables or flowers. Going to the park is fun. Next, get a pot and fill it with dirt. Make holes in the dirt and drop the seeds into the holes. My favorite fruit is a peach. Water the seeds and put the pot in the sun. Watch the seeds grow! I hope you can come.

1. What is the topic of the paragraph?_____

2. Cross out the details that are **not** about the topic.

What Is a Paragraph?
Topics and Details

Read the paragraphs and answer the questions.

> My family loves movies. We have movie night once a month. We choose a movie and make popcorn. I want new ice skates. We all watch the movie together.

1. What is the topic? _____
2. Cross out the detail that does **not** belong.

> Mario joined Little League. He got a new fishing pole. He was so excited to play baseball. His first time up, he hit the ball. He hit a home run!

3. What is the topic? _____
4. Cross out the detail that does **not** belong.

> Do you like games? Everyone has a favorite. Some like checkers. I like a tuna sandwich. Others like board games. I like computer games the best.

5. What is the topic? _____
6. Cross out the detail that does **not** belong.

Choose a Topic
Writing Process Chart

Look at the writing process chart. Notice that no matter where you are in the process, you can go back to rework or add to your writing before you move on to the next step.

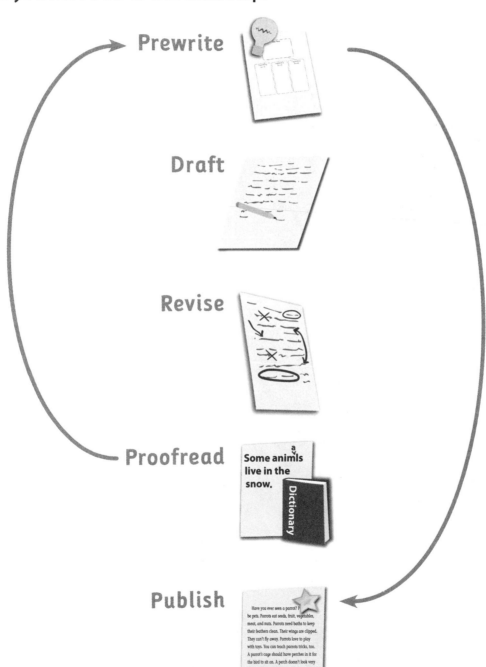

Choose a Topic
Find the Main Idea

Guided Exercises

> The **main idea** is the most important point in the paragraph. The **topic sentence** states the main idea.

 The topic of Winnie's Paragraph is animal homes.

- Find the sentence that states the main idea in the paragraph. Underline it.

Read the paragraphs and answer the questions.

> It is easy to start a fish tank. You will need a clean tank. You will need a filter to keep the water clean. Be sure to choose fish that get along.

1. What is the topic? _____

2. Underline the sentence that states the main idea.

> You need to get ready to go running. First, you need sneakers that are made for running. You need loose clothing that moves easily. You need to drink water.

3. What is the topic? _____

4. Underline the sentence that states the main idea.

Choose a Topic
Plan Your Paragraph

Copy the ideas you brainstormed onto the lines provided. Choose
one of the topics to write about and write it in the space below. Then,
write the main idea that you will write about in your paragraph.

Brainstorming topics _____

_____

_____

My topic _____

_____

My main idea _____

_____

_____

_____

Create Supporting Details
Add Supporting Details

Guided Exercises

Supporting details give reasons for the main idea of a paragraph. You can use a graphic organizer to plan supporting details.

▶ **Winnie made a graphic organizer to plan her paragraph. She wrote her main idea and planned supporting details.**

- Point to the main idea.
- Point to a supporting detail.

What other supporting details could you add to a paragraph with this main idea? Add them to the graphic organizer. Look at Winnie's Paragraph if you need ideas.

```
                    Main Idea
        there are many kinds of animal homes
```

Supporting Detail	Supporting Detail	Supporting Detail
in trees		

Create Supporting Details
Paragraph Graphic Organizer

Write the main idea for your paragraph in the top box.
Add supporting details in the other boxes.

Main Idea

Supporting Detail	Supporting Detail	Supporting Detail

Draft a Paragraph
Ideas to Sentences

Guided Exercises

The purpose of **drafting** is to write ideas in clear, complete sentences.

▶ **Winnie started drafting by turning each detail in the graphic organizer into a complete sentence.**

▶ **Detail: in trees**

- Sentence: Animals live in trees or inside caves.

▶ **Detail: below the ground**

- Sentence: Other animals live below the ground.
- Point to the capital letter and the end mark. Is this a complete sentence?

Write your own sentence for the following details from Winnie's graphic organizer.

1. Detail: inside caves

_____

_____

2. Detail: in the ocean

_____

_____

What Is a Pronoun?
Miss Muffet Pronouns

Guided Exercises

> A **pronoun** is a word that takes the place of a noun. Some pronouns are *I*, *me*, *you*, *he*, *she*, *it*, *him*, and *her*.

▶ **Miss Muffet was sitting. A spider sat down beside (her.)**

Whom did the spider sit beside? The word is circled. This **pronoun** takes the place of the noun *Miss Muffet*.

▶ **It scared Miss Muffet.**

What scared Miss Muffet? Circle the word. This pronoun takes the place of the noun spider.

Underline the pronoun that can take the place of the underlined word or words.

1. Tom took us fishing.   (He,   She,   It)

2. The bobber went under.   (Me,   You,   It)

3. I grabbed the rod from Tom.   (me,   her,   him)

4. Suzy got the net.   (He,   She,   Me)

5. The fish pulled hard.   (I,   It,   You)

What Is a Pronoun?

Pick the Pronoun

Underline the pronoun or pronouns in the sentence.

1. He is always late.

2. Can you take me to the movies?

3. She painted it.

Choose the correct pronoun in the sentence.

4. (I,   Him) went to the science fair with Jo.

5. (She,   Me) made a robot.

6. (Me,   It) could walk and pick up tools.

7. Bo asked (I,   her) for help.

Rewrite this sentence using a pronoun. Pretend you were the soccer player.

8. Anna played soccer. _____

Plural Pronouns
We, Us, You, They, Them

Guided Exercises

A **plural pronoun** is a word that takes the place of a plural noun. Some plural pronouns are *we*, *us*, *you*, *they*, and *them*.

▶ **John eats cookies. They are good with milk.**

- What does John eat? Underline it. This word is a plural noun.
- What word in the second sentence takes the place of plural noun? Circle it. This word is a plural pronoun.

Circle the plural pronoun that takes the place of the underlined word or words.

1. Max has <u>rabbits</u>. Max gives them carrots.

2. <u>Hank and Isabel</u> hid. They were in the fort.

3. <u>Mack and I</u> are friends. We play together.

4. Juan called <u>Dan and me</u>. He asked us to come over.

5. Ruffy licks <u>Liz and you</u>. Ruffy likes both of you.

Plural Pronouns

Pronouns for More Than One

Circle the pronoun that takes the place of the underlined words.

1. <u>Hank and I</u> play in the park.   (We,   He)

2. Joe met <u>Tim, Randy, and Jill</u>.   (her,   them)

3. <u>Tigers and lions</u> pace back and forth.   (We,   They)

4. Sal and Ann talk to <u>the cooks</u>.   (it,   them)

5. Give the tickets to <u>my friends and me</u>.   (us,   you)

Write the pronoun that completes the sentence.

6. Hi. _____ are Zack and Winnie.   (We,   He)

7. Can you take _____ to see our friends?   (you,   us)

8. _____ live ten miles from here.   (Us,   They)

9. Will _____ drive there?   (me,   you)

10. We want to see _____ .   (them,   us)

More Pronouns
Special Pronouns

Guided Exercises

Use a **possessive pronoun** to talk about things that belong to someone. Use a special pronoun to refer to someone who has already been named in a sentence.

▶ **Anna buttoned her coat.**

- Who owns the coat?
- Circle the word that replaces the name of the coat's owner. This word is a **possessive pronoun**.

▶ **Anna baked herself some cookies.**

- Point to the noun at the beginning of the sentence.
- Circle the pronoun that refers to that person.

Circle the pronoun that tells who owns the bat.

1. That is my <u>bat</u>.

2. The black <u>bat</u> is also mine.

Underline the special pronoun.

3. Kevin wrote a note to himself.

More Pronouns

Pronoun Practice

Choose a word from the word bank to complete the sentence.

> myself   yourself   himself   herself   ourselves

1. Jeremy rode the horse by _____ .

2. Mrs. Adams drove _____ to Texas.

3. We stayed in the tent by _____ .

Choose a word from the word bank to complete the sentence.

> your   yours   his   her   mine

4. The ice cream belongs to me. The ice cream is _____ .

5. These goats belong to you. These goats are _____ .

6. The grapes belong to Mr. Cane. The grapes are _____ .

7. This ring belongs to Sue. This is _____ ring.

8. This raincoat belongs to you. This is _____ raincoat.

Revise Your Draft: Introductions

Alexander's First Draft

Use Alexander's first draft as you work through the lessons in the unit.

Have you ever seen a parrot? Parrots can be pets. Parrots eat seeds, fruit, vegetables, meat, and nuts. Parrots need baths to keep their feathers clean. Their wings are clipped. They can't fly away. Parrots love to play with toys. You can teach parrots tricks, too. A parrot's cage should have perches in it for the bird to sit on. A perch doesn't look very comfortable. A parrot can learn to step onto your finger. I have a green parrot, and he loves nuts.

Revise Your Draft: Introductions
Strong Beginning and Topic Sentences

Guided Exercises

A **beginning sentence** introduces a paragraph, tells what it is about, and gets the reader's attention. Sometimes the beginning sentence is the same as the **topic sentence**.

▶ **Alexander's beginning sentence: Have you ever seen a parrot?**

- How does this sentence get your attention?

▶ **Alexander's topic sentence: Parrots can be pets.**

- Does this sentence tell you what the paragraph is about?

Read each pair of sentences. Circle the stronger topic sentence.

1. A dog can be your best friend.   Dogs are nice.

2. Hamsters are cute.   Hamsters are playful animals.

Read Alexander's First Draft again. Write a stronger topic sentence for Alexander's First Draft and mark the changes on the draft.

3. _____

_____

Revise Your Draft: Introductions
Revise the Beginning Sentence and Topic Sentence

Use your draft paragraph to answer the questions. When you are finished, mark your changes directly on the first draft of your paragraph.

1. Do you have a strong beginning sentence that introduces your topic and catches the reader's attention?

    A. Yes   **B.** No

2. Write a stronger beginning sentence for your paragraph.

    _____

    _____

3. Does your topic sentence tell your main idea?

    A. Yes   **B.** No

4. What can you add to make your topic sentence stronger?

    _____

    _____

5. Revise your topic sentence.

    _____

WRITING SKILLS

Get from Point to Point: Transitions
Transition Words List

Use these transitions as you work through the lessons.

Time

before	soon	then	after	finally
first	next	meanwhile	later	last

Cause and Effect

because	if . . . then	so
for	since	therefore

Importance

most of all	mainly	finally	least of all
mostly	as well	lastly	

Relationships

also	but	instead	too
although	for example	on the other hand	yet
besides	however	such as	

Place

above	below	inside	there
across	far	near	within
around	here	outside	

Get from Point to Point: Transitions
Use Transitions

Guided Exercises

A **transition** is a word or phrase that connects one sentence to another. Transitions help sentences flow and show relationships among ideas.

▶ **Parrots love to play with toys. You can teach parrots tricks, too.**

What word connects these sentences from Alexander's First Draft? Circle it.

Choose a transition word to complete the sentence.

1. Toe shoes help ballerinas dance well, _____, they can make their feet hurt.

2. Tap shoes have metal on the bottom. _____ they make tapping sounds.

Add a transition and rewrite these sentences from Alexander's First Draft.

3. Their wings are clipped. They can't fly away.

_____

_____

Get from Point to Point: Transitions
Add Transitions to Your Draft

Follow these steps to add transitions to your first draft.

1. Read your paragraph aloud.

2. Do all of your ideas connect from one sentence to the other?

   A. Yes

   B. No

3. Does the order of all of your sentences make sense?

   A. Yes

   B. No

4. Find transition words that you can use in your paragraph. List them here.

   _____

   _____

   _____

5. Add the transitions to your draft.

WRITING SKILLS

Write a Conclusion
What's a Conclusion?

Guided Exercises

A **concluding sentence** is the last sentence of a paragraph. It sums up or restates the main idea of the paragraph.

 Alexander's main idea: Parrots can be pets.

 Alexander's concluding sentence: I have a green parrot, and he loves nuts.

- What's wrong with Alexander's concluding sentence?

Circle the best concluding sentence for the paragraph.

1. Football can be a rough game. Players wear special clothing to help them stay safe. They wear thick pads and helmets, too.

    A. Football players have to be careful so they don't get hurt.

    B. They wear special shoes, too.

2. Basketball is great to watch. The best players are very tall. They jump up and toss the ball through the hoop.

    A. I like to play every afternoon.

    B. Basketball players make it look easy.

3. Write a new concluding sentence for Alexander's First Draft. Mark the revision on the draft.

Write a Conclusion
Write a Concluding Sentence

Reread your draft. Focus on your concluding sentence.

1. Does your conclusion restate the main idea of the paragraph?

   A. Yes

   B. No

2. Are there different words you can use so the concluding sentence is not the same as the topic sentence?

   A. Yes

   B. No

3. Write or revise your concluding sentence.

   _____

   _____

   _____

4. Mark the final changes directly on your first draft.

Revise for Content

Fix Content

Guided Exercises

Revising means rewriting. The purpose of revising is to improve your writing.

▶ **When you revise, delete details that don't belong, look for ideas that you might move or rewrite, and add more details.**

- Look at Alexander's First Draft and draw a line through the sentence that is not about the main idea of the paragraph.

- Find the sentence in Alexander's First Draft that should be moved. Circle it.

Use Alexander's First Draft to complete the exercises.

1. Circle two sentences that would be good to add to Alexander's First Draft.

   A. Baths also keep the bird's skin from getting too dry.

   B. I also like to play chess and do word puzzles.

   C. You can also teach your parrot how to speak.

   D. My friend Johnny has two kittens.

2. Mark any revisions directly on Alexander's First Draft.

Revise for Content

Revise Your Ideas

Reread your draft. Focus on revising your ideas.

1. Are there any details in your paragraph that do not say something about the main idea?

    A. Yes

    B. No

2. If you answered *Yes*, cross out those details.

3. Are there any sentences that would sound better somewhere else in the paragraph?

    A. Yes

    B. No

4. Circle those sentences and draw an arrow to where they should go.

5. Are there any ideas you could add to your writing?

    A. Yes

    B. No

6. Write any new sentences on your paragraph.

Revise a Paragraph
Revising Checklist

Use this checklist to revise your paragraph. Check off what you have already done. Keep revising until you can check off everything.

- ☐ Is there an interesting beginning sentence?

- ☐ Does the topic sentence state the main idea?

- ☐ Do all the sentences tell about the main idea?

- ☐ Did I add details about the main idea?

- ☐ Did I delete details that are not about the main idea?

- ☐ Are the sentences written in an order that makes sense?

- ☐ Are there transition words to connect ideas?

- ☐ Are there transitions to make the sentences flow from one to the other?

- ☐ Is there a strong concluding sentence?

WRITING SKILLS

Revise a Paragraph
Revise Your First Draft

Use this space to rewrite your draft paragraph, including your revisions.

_____

_____

_____

_____

_____

_____

_____

_____

_____

WRITING SKILLS

_____

_____

_____

_____

_____

_____

_____

_____

_____

_____

_____

LANGUAGE ARTS ORANGE

Revise a Paragraph

Tell Me About My Paragraph

Have another person read your revised paragraph and answer these questions.

1. Does the paragraph have a main idea?

   _____

2. Does the topic sentence express the main idea?

   _____

3. Do all the sentences in the paragraph support or relate to the main idea?

   _____

4. Are there details to support the main idea?

   _____

5. Are there sentences or ideas that do not relate to the main idea? If so, what are they?

   _____

6. Are the sentences written in an order that makes sense? Why or why not?

   _____

7. Do the sentences flow from one to the other?
    Why or why not?

    _____

8. Are transition words used to connect sentences?

    _____

9. Is there a strong concluding sentence?

    _____

10. How could the writing be improved?

    _____

    _____

    _____

Semester Review: Sentences, Nouns, and Verbs

Practice Makes Perfect

Choose the answer.

1. Which is a complete sentence?

   A. Plays the banjo.

   B. likes the way it sounds

   C. Steve loves music.

2. Which is a complete sentence?

   A. gave a gift

   B. Her friends sang a song.

   C. Ella's party began at

3. Which is a complete sentence?

   A. The fire engine roared

   B. the cars got out of the way.

   C. I covered my ears.

What kind of sentence is this? Choose the answer.

4. We are hungry.

   A. statement   C. exclamation

   B. question   D. command

5. Is it lunch time yet?

   A. statement   C. exclamation

   B. question   D. command

6. Put these spoons on the table.

   A. statement   C. exclamation

   B. question   D. command

7. Let's eat right away!

   A. statement   C. exclamation

   B. question   D. command

Write the noun from the word bank in the correct column.

Florida   jacket   dentist

Person	Place	Thing
8.	9.	10.

WRITING SKILLS

What kind of noun is this? Write *C* for common noun or *P* for proper noun.

11. ____ Joey

12. ____ store

13. ____ tiger

14. ____ Sky Lake

Find the noun from the word bank that needs a capital letter. Write it correctly on the line.

> mug   ocean   day   thursday

15. _____

Circle the verb in the sentence.

16. My sister plays softball.

17. That tree is tall.

Which underlined word is a verb? Choose the answer.

18. <u>Eric</u> <u>likes</u> vanilla <u>ice cream</u>.

    A. Eric

    B. likes

    C. ice cream

Semester Review: Letters, Nouns, Subjects & Verbs, and Pronouns

Practice Makes Perfect

Circle the answer.

1. Choose the correct heading.

   862 Salem Avenue   862 Salem avenue
   Dayton, Ohio 45406   Dayton, OH 45406
   May 6, 2010   May 6 2010

2. Choose the correct greeting.

   A. dear Mrs. Sands!   **C.** Dear mrs. Sands

   B. Dear Mrs. Sands,   **D.** Dear Mrs. Sands

3. Choose the correct closing.

   A. your friend,   **C.** Your friend,

   B. Your friend   **D.** Your Friend

Mark the answers correctly.

4. Circle the singular nouns. Underline the plural nouns.

   star   doors   cherries   shoe

Choose the answer.

5. Which sentence is correct?

   A. Do mouses really like cheese?

   B. Do mice really like cheese?

WRITING SKILLS

6. Which sentence is correct?

   A. Brush your teeth before bed.

   B. Brush your tooths before bed.

7. Which sentence is correct?

   A. The sun shine.

   B. The sun shines.

8. Which sentence is correct?

   A. Ten people sing.

   B. Ten people sings.

Circle the subject. Underline the verb.

9. The dog barks.

Choose the best pronoun to replace the underlined noun.

10. <u>Todd</u> collects baseball cards.

    A. It   **B.** He   **C.** She

11. <u>The cards</u> are worth a lot of money.

    A. They   **B.** Them   **C.** It

12. They are worth more than <u>Anna's</u> stamps.

    A. your   **B.** my   **C.** her

© K12 Inc. All rights reserved.

What Is Proofreading?

Ron's Paragraph

Use Ron's paragraph as you work through the lessons in the unit.

Evry summer I set up a Lemonade stand. it has a nice sign on it. The sign say, "Yummy lemonade 25 cents a cup." I painted yellow lemons on the sign myself. I fill cups with lemonade and some ice cube. People buy the lemonade? Make a lot of money. It's luckie I love math. math helps me because have to make change. I want to start mine own business when I grows up?

WRITING SKILLS

What Is Proofreading?
How to Proofread

WRITING SKILLS

Guided Exercises

You can use **proofreading marks** to correct sentences.

 Ron's first sentences: Evry summer I set up a Lemonade stand. it has a nice sign on it.

- Use slashes to fix the errors in the sentence.
- Use carets to add any new words or letters.

These sentences contain errors in punctuation or grammar, or they are missing a word. Correct the errors using proofreading marks. Finally, correct the mistakes in Ron's Paragraph.

1. it has a nice sign on it.

_____

2. I fill cups with lemonade and some ice cube.

_____

3. People buy the lemonade?

_____

4. Make a lot of money.

_____

Use a Dictionary
How to Use a Dictionary

Guided Exercises

A **dictionary** contains words with their definitions, in alphabetical order. **Guide words** are the two words at the top of a dictionary page that show you the first and last words on each page.

 The word "Evry" in Ron's first sentence is misspelled.

- Use a **dictionary**. Look up the word to spell it correctly.
- What does the word mean?

Use a dictionary to find the answer.

1. What is the correct spelling of the word *towil*? _____

2. Write the syllables in the word *active*. _____

3. How do you pronounce the word *myth*? _____

4. What part of speech is the word *perform*? _____

5. What does the word *around* mean? _____

6. Choose the word that would be on the page with the guide words *big—bill*.

   A. beg   **B.** bid   **C.** build   **D.** bike

Use a Dictionary
Look It Up

Use a dictionary to look up each word. Then, complete the puzzle.

| guest | rest | soar | yet | soggy |

Across

1. to fly upward

3. visitor

4. even; still

Down

1. soaked; very wet

2. sleep; stop

Use a Thesaurus

Sample Thesaurus

Use this sample thesaurus as you work through the lessons in the unit.

remain–reward

remain *verb*
Synonym: stay
Antonym: move

repair *verb*
Synonyms: fix, mend
Antonym: break

repeat *verb*
Synonyms: say, recite, quote, redo
Antonym: say once

rest *verb*
Synonyms: relax, doze, sleep, nap, be still, be quiet
Antonyms: work, move

return *verb*
Synonym: visit
Antonyms: avoid, keep

reward *noun*
Synonyms: prize, award, bonus, tip
Antonym: punishment

Use a Thesaurus

How to Use a Thesaurus

Guided Exercises

> A **thesaurus** is a reference work that gives synonyms and antonyms for words.

 Ron's second sentence: it has a nice sign on it.

- Use a **thesaurus** to find a better synonym for "nice." Mark changes on Ron's Paragraph.

Use a thesaurus to replace the underlined words with synonyms. Create whacky nursery rhymes.

Twinkle, twinkle, little star,
How I wonder what you are!

Row, row, row your boat,
Gently down the stream.

Humpty Dumpty sat on a wall,
Humpty Dumpty had a great fall.

Use a Checklist

Use the Checklist

Guided Exercises

A **checklist** helps a writer find and correct errors in grammar, spelling, punctuation, and capitalization.

The town are holding a poster contest. The poster has to show how we can help others.

- Use the Writer's Checklist to check these sentences. Correct the error.

My poster is almost finished. Me have to color the picture.

- Use the Writer's Checklist to check these sentences. Correct the error.

Use the Writer's Checklist to find and correct errors. There is one error in each sentence.

> Mine poster shows how we can help others. My clubs' name would be "The Helping Hands." adults and kids can sign up to help others. Each persons who joins can choose a way to help. Adults can shop for peeple who are sick. Kids can rake leave or shovel snow. Together we can help our neighbors?

_____

_____

_____

_____

_____

_____

 .Reward. . . . .

Draw a picture to illustrate your paragraph.

Publish Your Work

Tell Me About My Paragraph

Have another person read your revised paragraph and answer these questions.

1. Does the paragraph have a main idea? What is it?

   _____

2. Is there a topic sentence that expresses the main idea? Write it here.

   _____

3. Do all the sentences in the paragraph support the main idea? If not, which don't?

   _____

4. Does the paragraph have a title? What is it?

   _____

5. Are the sentences error-free?

   _____

6. What could the writer have done to improve this paragraph?

   _____

   _____

7. Which words were the most interesting and colorful to read?

_____

8. Is the writing neat and easy to read?

_____

9. State one way the writing can be improved.

_____